Contents

Spurgeon's Sermons on
Old Testament Women

Book One

CHARLES HADDON SPURGEON

kregel
PUBLICATIONS

Grand Rapids, MI 49501

Spurgeon's Sermons on Old Testament Women • Book One
by Charles H. Spurgeon.

Copyright © 1994 by Kregel Publications.

Published by Kregel Publications, a division of Kregel, Inc.,
P.O. Box 2607, Grand Rapids, MI 49501. Kregel
Publications provides trusted, biblical publications for
Christian growth and service. Your comments and sug-
gestions are valued.

Cover artwork: Don Ellens
Cover and book design: Alan G. Hartman

Library of Congress Cataloging-in-Publication Data

Spurgeon, C. H. (Charles Haddon), 1834–1892.
   [Sermons on Old Testament women]
   Spurgeon's Sermons on Old Testament Women / by
Charles H. Spurgeon.
      p.   cm.
   1. Women in the Bible—Sermons. 2. Bible. O.T.—
Sermons. 3. Sermons, American. I. Title. II. Series:
Spurgeon, C. H. (Charles Haddon), 1834–1892. C. H.
Spurgeon sermon series.
BS575.S58   1994   221.9'22'082—dc20   94-7831
                                                    CIP
ISBN 0-8254-3781-4 (pbk.)

           1 2 3 4 5 printing / year 98 97 96 95 94

1

*Esther's Exaltation**

*Then Mordecai commanded to answer Esther, Think not with thyself
that thou shalt escape in the king's house, more than all the Jews.
For if thou altogether holdest thy peace at this time, then shall there
enlargement and deliverance arise to the Jews from another place;
but thou and thy father's house shall be destroyed: and who knoweth
whether thou art come to the kingdom for such a time as this?
(Esther 4:13–14).*

The appeal of Mordecai in his pressing time of distress was to one
single person, namely, to Esther. I believe that I shall do better this
morning by making my sermon an address to individuals than by
speaking of nations or churches. I assuredly believe that our nation has
been raised up and brought to her present unique position that she may be
the means of spreading the gospel throughout all the nations of the earth.
I judge that God has blessed the two great nations of the Anglo-Saxon
race—England and the United States—and given them pre-eminence in
commerce and in liberty on purpose that in such a time as this they may
spread abroad the knowledge of the glory of God in the face of Jesus
Christ.

Woe to these nations if they fail to fulfill their solemn obligations! If,
being raised up for a purpose, they refuse to perform it, they shall melt
away. If, being armed and carrying weapons, they turn back in the day of
battle, both will perish as surely did the power of Macedon and the domin-
ion of Rome. We ought to be very careful as a people to act upon the rule
of righteousness and the principles of peace; for any other conduct is incon-
sistent with our high calling. We are entrusted with great opportunities; if
we do not rightly use them the New Zealander of Macaulay may yet sur-
vey the ruins of this empire-city. "You and your father's house shall be

* This sermon is taken from *The Metropolitan Tabernacle Pulpit* and was
preached on Sunday morning, April 27, 1884.

destroyed," said Mordecai to Esther, and he says the same to us. Oh, that our nation may know the day of her visitation.

We might properly say of any Christian church that it has its own appointed place in the purposes of divine mercy. If the candle is lighted, even though it be set upon a golden candlestick, it is not lighted for itself, but that it may give light to all who are in the house. If any church fails to bless others, and so proves unfaithful to her solemn trust, the Lord will take away the candlestick out of its place, and leave the unfaithful to mourn in darkness. Remember the Lord's warning voice, "Go ye now unto my place which was in Shiloh, where I set my name at the first, and see what I did to it for the wickedness of my people Israel" (Jer. 7:12). Remember, also, unfaithful Jerusalem, whose house is left unto her desolate because she obeyed not the voice of the Lord. The church in Rome was once a church of high commanding influence for good: you know what it has become. Some other churches are on the way, I fear, to the same dreadful end. God grant that none of the churches with which we are connected as Christian people may ever either apostatize from the faith, or grow lax and worldly, or become indifferent to the glory of God and the salvation of men. I might thus speak to each church and say, "Who knows whether you are come to the kingdom for such a time as this?"

Beloved, it is a wonderfully easy thing to denounce the faults of a government or of a nation, to complain of this being done, and of that being left undone; and this amusement may only serve to divert our conscience from its more profitable duties at home. But consider the matter, and remember that in a free state we each one are part and parcel of the nation, and of the government; and we are each one personally responsible in our measure and degree for all the acts of the nation. It is an easy matter to tie up our country to the stocks like a criminal and then to flagellate it without mercy; it would be a far more profitable business to use the whip of criticism upon ourselves.

The same is true with regard to a church. People are too apt to condemn in the mass what they tolerate in themselves as individuals. But why are we so ready to accuse the churches? Why are we so censorious as to what the churches do, and what the churches are? Who make up the churches? Why, we each one by our influence help to make the churches good, or bad, or indifferent, as the case may be.

Therefore, I will not waste time in generalities, but I will come to personalities. I will follow Mordecai's tack, and speak alone to Esther; that is to say, to each one who may happen to be here to whom God has entrusted opportunity, talent, and position. I would urge them to remember that there is a something for each believer to do, a work which he cannot delegate to another, a task which it is his privilege to be permitted to undertake, which it will be to his solemn disgrace and detriment if he do not execute, but which will be to his eternal glory under God if he be found faithful in it. The gospel assures us that the great householder has committed talents "to every man according to his several ability." Our hope of success this morning in our sermon shall lie in your individualizing yourselves and hearing the voice of the Spirit of God, saying to each one, "Who know whether *you* art come to the kingdom for such a time as this?"

I shall lay out my sermon in four parcels, arranging it under four words. I. The first word is

Hearken!

Hearken to my word, as Mordecai desired Esther to hearken to him. Hearken while God the Lord speaks to your heart, and calls you to your high vocation.

Hearken, first, to a question. Beloved, *will you separate your interests from those of your people and your God?* I do not think that Mordecai was afraid that Esther would do so; but still it is sometimes as well to prevent an evil before we perceive it; and he did so by saying, "Think not with thyself that thou shalt escape in the king's house." It was possible that being a queen it might enter into her mind that she would be safe even if all the rest of the Jews were put to death.

It would be a painful thing that her countrymen should be destroyed, but still the stroke might not touch her in the seclusion of the palace, where she had "not yet showed her kindred nor her people." She would still remain the favored wife of the great king; and she might, therefore, selfishly look to herself, and leave those who were in peril to look to themselves or to their God, while she coldly hoped that the Lord would somehow or other give them deliverance.

Does that temptation come across the path of any one of us? It may. You may say, "I shall be saved though the city should perish in its iniquity. Though the people are steeped in poverty and ignorance, I shall enjoy plenty and live in light. I know the Lord myself, and that is my main concern; if the heathen perish I am not one of them, and I am thankful that it will not interfere with my destiny."

Will you argue in this selfish manner? Will you follow the wicked policy of separating your own personal interests from those of your Redeemer and His church? If so your ship is wrecked before it leaves the harbor. You are no child of God if this principle holds the mastery over you. Your salvation lies not in your separation from Christ and His church, but in your union with them. Over the sea of life there is no passing in safety but in the vessel which carries your Lord and His disciples.

Are you going to sail in a separate boat, or will you try to swim across the sea in your own strength? Then look to yourself, and expect disaster. If your interests and Christ's are to be separated you must supply yourself with atonement, with righteousness, with spiritual life, and with heavenly food; yes, you must make a heaven for yourself. You cannot do this, and therefore it would be your ruin to attempt to stand alone. Do you wish to be joined with Jesus so as to be rescued from hell? I tell you, there is no receiving Christ unless you receive His doctrine and rule. You must receive this grace also, namely, that you give yourself to Him to make His interests your interests, His life your life, His kingdom your kingdom, His glory your glory. Your personal welfare will be found in submergence into Christ. Sink or swim with your Lord and His cause.

Do you mean to separate yourself from the church of God, and say, "I shall look to my own salvation, but I cannot be supposed to take an interest in saving others"? In such a spirit as that I do not say you *will* be lost, but I say you *are* lost already. It is as necessary that you be saved from selfishness as from any other vice. Some of our worst fetters are those which are forged by selfishness, and this is one of the chief bonds which our Redeemer must burst for us. We must live unto God and love others as God has loved us, or else we are still in the gall of bitterness and in the bonds of iniquity.

I conceive that nobody who professes to be a Christian would deliberately wish to set up a private estate apart from Christ and His cause. Then if you are partners in name, be partners in fact. If you have fellowship with Christ—remember that it is of the essence of fellowship that you are in co-partnership with Him; if He is a loser, you are a loser, and you are to fret about it; and if He is a gainer, you are a gainer, and you are to joy in that. He bids you rejoice with Him that He has found His sheep which was lost. I ask again, "Are you determined to set up a separate interest from Christ?" If you are, say so deliberately and count the cost. Mark that man; for though he may in his selfishness spread himself abroad and flourish like a green bay tree, yet the day shall come when he shall wither, and the place that knows him shall know him no more forever. O professed servant of God, minister, deacon, or private church-member, you shall perish if once you begin to live unto yourself. Remember that word, careless women, "She that liveth in pleasure is dead while she liveth"; and hearken, you selfish religionists, to this truth: "If ye live after the flesh ye shall die."

Hearken to a second question. *If you could separate your interests from those of the cause of God, would you thereby secure them?* You are a church-member: you think also that you are a living member of the body of Christ, and you are tempted to look to yourself and to leave others to their shifts. Notice—"Think not with thyself that thou shalt escape in the king's house, more than all the Jews." Is it so, that you enjoy all sorts of Christian privileges, you therefore harden your heart concerning dying churches and desponding saints? Do you imagine that the body can be sick, and yet you as a member of it will not suffer? I tell you, if the church of

God goes aside it will be to your injury; if the truth of God be not preached you will be a loser; if Christian life be not vigorous you will be weakened.

When an unhealthy atmosphere is over other Christians you will breathe it. Sinners cannot be left in their spiritual death without creating a foulness in the air which is to the peril of us all. If this great city is left to seethe and rot in its infidelity and misery and filthiness, don't think you Christian people will escape. You dwell with these outcasts, and you are already feeling their influence, and will feel it still more if they do not feel yours. How far and how deep that participation will go I will not venture to prophesy, for I am no prophet, neither the son of a prophet; but there are elements now fermenting which threaten, first, the existence of the commonwealth, and next, the liberties of Christian worship. Things cannot long remain as they are. This great flood of wretchedness must be assuaged, or it will sweep us all away.

I do not know what of evil may yet come of the negligence of the Christian church toward the population with which it is surrounded. Those wretched beings who starve in overcrowded rooms will not die unavenged if nothing more comes of it than the sin which is begotten of want. If you live in a house well-ventilated, and well-drained, and you have near you hovels foul, filthy, dilapidated, overcrowded, when the fever breeds there it will not respect your garden wall; it will come up into your windows, strike down your children, or lay you yourself in the grave.

As such mischief to health cannot be confined to the locality in which it was born, so is it with spiritual and moral disease; it must and will spread on all sides. This may be a selfish argument; but as we are battling with selfishness, we may fitly take Goliath's sword with which to cut off his head. You Christian people suffer if the church suffers; you suffer even if the world suffers. If you are not creating a holy warmth, the chill of sin is freezing you. Unconsciously the death which is all around will creep over you who are idle in the church, and it will soon paralyze all your energies unless in the name of God you arouse yourselves to give battle to it. You must unite with the Lord and His people in winning the victory over sin, or sin will win the victory over you. Listen to what I say, and let it sink into your mind.

Next, remember, for your humiliation, that *God can do without you.* Enlargement and deliverance will arise to His people from another place if it come not by us. If the Lord were tied up to anyone, or any one church, or any one nation, it were treasonable for that person, church, or nation to be negligent; but as the Lord waits not for man, neither tarries for the sons of men, it becomes them to mind what they are at.

He can do without *us.* When He looked and there was no one, His own arm brought salvation; and as it was of old so will it be again. Mark you that. The great Owner of the vineyard will have fruit at the end of the year, and if yonder tree does not bear it, He will cut it down: why does it cumber the ground? If the husbandmen consult their own gain, and plot to gain the inheritance for themselves, their lord will destroy them, "and will let out his vineyard unto other husbandmen, which shall render him the fruits in their seasons."

He will effect His purpose; He will fetch home His banished; He will gather together His scattered sheep; He will cause the earth to be full of the knowledge of the Lord as the waters cover the sea; and if we do not gather in the wanderers, or spread the knowledge of His grace, the work will be done by more faithful men. The Spirit says unto the church in Philadelphia, "Hold fast that which thou hast, that no man take thy crown." The crown of this church has been soul-winning: suffer none to rob you of it. If any one of you has gained already the high honor of bringing sinners to Christ, do not lose it by a future life of laziness or powerlessness. Hold fast your zeal and perseverance, that you may be rewarded at the last day.

He can do without you; remember that, O servant of the Lord! We are apt to think ourselves wonderfully important, and begin to fret if we are put aside from our work for a little; but perhaps this affliction is necessary to teach us and to teach all who know us to cease from man and to look to God alone. It would be a sad thing to exhibit pride and self-conceit, and provoke the Lord to show the world how readily He can dispense with our labors. With this truth in view my heart cries—

> Dismiss me not thy service, Lord,
> But train me for thy will.

Here follows a still more sobering reflection. Recollect that as God can do without us, *it may be He will do without us.* It might come to pass that God would say, "I will no more bless the world by this England; she has become selfishly mercantile; she cares more for commerce than for righteousness; she is drunken and infidel; I will give her up. Her merchants care nothing for the poor, whose labor is ill-requited; let her pass away as all oppressors must, and let the nations say—'Alas, alas, that great city, that mighty city! For in one hour so great riches is come to nought.'" He may say to any church, "Repent; or else I will come unto you quickly, and will fight against you with the sword of my mouth." "Ichabod" has been written aforetime, and may be again, on places where once there shone upon the forefront the inscription—"Holiness unto the Lord." So also any man may be set aside, even as the Lord put away Saul, and said to Him, "You have rejected the word of the Lord, and the Lord has rejected you from being king over Israel." Though, like Samson, a hero may have slain his thousands, and the hopes of Israel hang upon the hero; yet shorn and blinded, he may yet grind with slaves at the mill if his lusts enslave him. The Lord may decline to use us if we are not prepared in such a time as this to do our very utmost, and to lay ourselves out for the cause of truth and holiness. It may please the Lord to say of a wicked and slothful servant, "Take away his talent from him and give it to him who has ten talents." He may say to any pastor among us, "Let his habitation be desolate, and his bishopric let another take." Listen, I pray you, to this warning from the Lord. Hear, O heaven, and give ear, O earth, for the Lord will judge His people, and to whom much is given of him shall much be required.

Notice one thing more. *How ill you bear the disgrace, if ever it come upon you, of having suffered your golden opportunities to be wasted?* What if Israel had been destroyed for lack of Esther's intercession? Her name would have been a byword among other nations as a base and traitorous woman. If the people had been spared by some other means, and she had refused her mission, as long as there lived a Jew they would have kept no feast of Purim, but have cursed her memory. When I think of the neglects of our own ancestors I am anxious that we take warning by them.

Times do not tarry, and tides do not wait; and if we do not avail ourselves of them while they are with us, our descendants may lament our neglects. I fear that the best among us can recollect with regret times which we have suffered to pass over us unimproved. We can never call them back again.

You did not train your children: they are men and women now, and will not listen to you. Oh, parents, why did you not speak to them when they would have listened?

But what if a whole life should glide away in living for yourselves, in living for your own comfort and enriching? What if you have done nothing in all these years for the cause of the unfaithful servant! What dishonor awaits *you*! If you have been clouds without rain, wells without water, smoking lamps giving no light, fields that yield no harvest, what must be your portion?

Let every Esther resolve that she will never bring this ban upon her name: let every man, woman, and even child among us, knowing the lord, feel that the vows of the Lord are upon us, and that by imperative necessity we must serve according to our capacity the cause of God and truth. If we even perish through our zeal for the Lord of hosts it will be grand thus to lose our lives. Thus much for the word "Hearken." May the Spirit of God sanctify your hearts by His word. II. I change a little, and the call is now to—

Consider

Consider to what some of you have been advanced. You have been raised to salvation. You have been lifted from the dunghill and set among princes. I have uttered the word "salvation"; but what an infinity of goodness lies hidden there! In the music of that word all sweetnesses meet together. What are the obligations of one elected according to the foreknowledge of God, redeemed by the heart's blood of Christ, and quickened by the Holy Spirit? What manner of persons ought we to be? You have been raised to that honor, walk worthy of it.

Besides that, some of you have been raised to a considerable degree of Christian knowledge—you are not now mere babes in grace; you are well instructed, and you have had a blessed experience both of trouble and of joy, which has made you strong in the Lord, and has confirmed you in the faith, and has admitted you into the inner circle where the joy of the Lord is best known.

If I had said that you had been elevated to be queens, like Esther, it would have been a poor elevation compared with that which you have actually received. Some of you who are the favorites of heaven have leaned your head on Christ's bosom, and have been permitted to sit where angels would wish to be; you are near and dear to Jesus, and espoused to Him in love.

In addition to all this, the Lord has raised some of you out of poverty and brought you to comparative wealth, perhaps to positive wealth; and He has given you positions which once you never dreamed of. To this He adds domestic comfort, and health, and prosperity in all its forms. The Lord has also given you talent. I fear we have all of us more ability than we use— but some have more talent than they themselves are aware of, and this perhaps they display in business, but never in the cause of God.

Thus you are brought to the kingdom; but why is it so? I want you to consider *why the Lord has brought you where you are.* Do you think he has done it for your own sake? Does he intend all this merely that you may practice self-indulgence? Can this be the design of God? Do not think so. Has He done all this merely to give you pleasure? Not so: God's work is like a net of many meshes, and these are all connected with each other. We are links of the same chain, and cannot move without moving others. We are members of one body, and God acts toward us with that fact in view.

He does not bless the hand for the hand's sake, but for the sake of the whole body. Well then, dear friend, you are confirmed in the faith that you may confirm others; talents are allotted to you that you may turn them over and bring in heavenly interest for your Lord. Whatever you have is yours not to hoard for yourself, or to spend upon yourself, but that you may use it as a good steward of God. Who knows whether you are come to the kingdom which God has given you for such a time as this, when there is need of you and all that is yours?

Consider, next, *at what a time it is that you have been thus advanced.* You have been instructed in the faith in a time when unbelief is rampant. What for? You have been confirmed in full assurance at a time when many are weak and trembling. What for? You have been entrusted with talent in a time when multitudes are perishing for lack of knowledge. What for? You are found in the church when others are dying or moving off. Why is this? You have wealth when many are starving. Why is this? You hold a high position when many master spirits are leading men into infidelity, or ritualism, or communism.

Why are you placed where you are? Beloved, your inevitable answer must be that God has put you where you are for some good purpose, which purpose must be connected with His own glory, and with the extension of His kingdom in the world. If, however, you think it enough to have secured a fortune, let me ask you—Do you think you are the proprietor of what you have amassed; or do you admit that you are a steward? If you are a steward, do not use the goods entrusted to you for your own ends, but for your Master; for if you do not, you are a thief. Whenever a steward considers that the estate is his own property, and not his master's, he is a thief, and before long his master will deal with him and say, "Give an account of your stewardship; for you may be no longer steward."

Consider also, I pray you, *under what very special circumstances you have come where you are.* To you as an individual I distinctly speak, and to no one else. It was a very strange thing that Esther, who was the foster child of Mordecai, a humble Jew, should rise from lowly rank to be the queen of Persia. Out of all the women gathered from every province how singular that she should be chosen to be queen!

Special Providence selected the Jewish maiden for the throne. The same is true of each one of us now occupying a post of usefulness. David was taken from the sheepfolds, from following the ewes great with young, that he might be the shepherd of God's people Israel. I am marveling to find myself where I now am; are not you? How came you into your present pastorate, my dear brother in the ministry? How did you gain that comfortable position which you now occupy in society? How came you even to be in the church of God? Oh, if anybody had told yonder brother a few years ago that he would be here, he would have sworn at them; but here he is, sitting at the feet of Jesus, charmed to be His disciple.

Now, consider what a wonder of grace you are, what a singular favor it is that you are where you are. Should not these remarkable dealings of the Lord toward you bind you to the divine service? Many a businessman here today obtaining a satisfactory livelihood has a dozen times been within an inch of bankruptcy, and yet he has obtained help, and passed the rock in safety. Some of you have been well-nigh ruined several times; and yet you still have bread to eat and raiment to put on. It is a miracle in your eyes that you have not come to beggary. Let your special deliverances and memorable mercies be as the tongue of persuasion, constraining you to grateful service. Consider how great things the Lord has done for you, and let us not have to say, "Many times did He deliver them, but they soon forgot His works. They understood not His wonders in Egypt; they remembered not the multitude of His mercies."

Then I beg you to consider once more, *with what singular personal adaptations you are endowed for the work to which God has called you.* I believe you are endowed with special capacity for a certain work, so that no one is as fitted for it as yourself: you are a key to a lock which no other key will fit so well. God has prepared you for the work for which you are appointed. Is it not written—"Also unto you, O Lord, belongs mercy: for you render to every man according to his work"? Each laborer for the Lord has his proper tools around him. God does not, like Pharaoh, require us to make bricks without straw, nor to fight without weapons, nor to build without a trowel. The Lord provides lamps, and oil, and wedding-garments for all who are called to the Bridegroom's midnight banquet. You, my brother, are equipped for such work as the Lord has appointed you; will you not at once get to your post? You say, "If I could preach, I would do it gladly." You would not preach worthily unless you are even now prepared to do other service for which you are fitted. You would be a disgrace to the pulpit if you are useless in the home circle.

If God entrusts you with a single talent, and you do not use it, neither would you use ten talents; for he who is unfaithful in that which is least, would be unfaithful in that which is greatest.

"But," says one, "I can hardly get out to public worship; I am a mother shut in at home with five or six little children." To you there is a little kingdom in your own household. No one can bring up those little ones for the Lord so well as you can. Your influence over them is as strong as it is tender. Now, do not say, "Because I am not allowed to be a preaching woman, therefore I will not attend to the lowly care of my children." It is far better to train your family for Jesus than to be attempting a work to which you are not called.

Let each one of you feel that he has come to his own little kingdom for such a time as this. You and your work fit each other: God has joined you together, let no man put you asunder. Ask for more power from the Holy Spirit, and if there happens to be a tool which the Lord intends for you which hangs a little higher than your present reach, get the ladder of earnest endeavor and you will soon attain it. Consider how you can improve yourself; give yourself to reading; study Scripture more, and use all helps toward increased knowledge and efficiency. If a further qualification be within your reach, be eager for it, and even the reaching after it may be as great a blessing to you as the talent itself. III. Thirdly,

Aspire

"Who knows whether you are come to the kingdom for such a time as this?" Rise to the utmost possible height. Fulfill your calling to its loftiest degree. Not only do all that you are sure you can do, but aim at something which as yet is high up among the questions. Say to yourself, "Who knows?" That is what the ambitious person says when he aspires to be great. When Louis Napoleon was shut up in the fortress of Ham, and everybody ridiculed his foolish attempts upon France, yet he said to himself, "Who knows? I am the nephew of my uncle, and may yet sit upon the imperial throne," and he did so before many years had passed.

I have no desire to make anyone ambitious after the poor thrones, and honors, and riches of this world; but I deeply desire to make you all ardently ambitious to honor God and bless men. Who knows? Does anybody know what God may do by you? Does anybody know what capacities slumber within your heart? I suggest the inquiry, and I will help you to an answer.

"Who knows whether you are come to the kingdom for such a time as this?" *Nobody knows to the contrary.* I cannot tell but what God may bless you to this entire nation. Nobody will dare to say that He cannot. I cannot tell but what God may bless you, my friend, to that part of the world in which you live, even though you may be deeply conscious of its great needs, and of your own insufficiency. Who can tell what the Lord can or will do? Dear mother, who knows but what the Lord Jesus may bless you to all the members of your family, so that by your means all the little ones shall come to Him? Nobody has any right to speak to the contrary. Who knows but what God may bless you, dear teacher, to all your Sunday school class, so that you may meet them all in heaven? Nobody can declare that it shall not be so, therefore strive after it. The watchword is, "Aspire."

Further, *nobody knows the limit of the possibilities which surround any man—should God please to use him.* "Alas," cries one, "I am soon at the end of my powers." My dear friend, if you begin calculating how much there is in you by nature, and how much you can do of yourself, you may as well end the inquiry by hearing our Lords word—"Without me you can do nothing." Though you be no better than a mere cipher, yet the Lord can make something of you. Set one before a cipher and it is ten directly. Let two or three noughts combine to serve the Lord, and if the Lord heads them these nothings become tens of thousands. Who knows what you can do?

Shall the church ever say, "Here is a problem we cannot solve?" Bite your lip through rather than have it thought that you doubt the power of the Almighty. All things are possible to him who believes. You are able to possess the land, the Lord being your helper. Go up against even these entrenched Canaanites, the walls of whose cities reach to heaven, for you can drive them out. You seem in your own sight to be as grasshoppers when compared with the sons of Anak; but the Lord on high is mighty, and out of the weakest things He hath ordained strength to His honor and glory.

Young man, I trust you have given your heart to the Lord; what are you going to do? You have come into some property unexpectedly; or you are promoted in a house of business—what is the meaning of it? "Who knows whether you are come to the kingdom for such a time as this?" My talented friend, should you not take your share in battling with present evils? I believe that in dark times God is making lamps with which to remove the gloom.

John Calvin is quietly studying when false doctrine is most rife, and he will be heard of at Geneva. A young man is here this morning—I do not know whereabouts he is, but I pray the Lord to make this to be an ordination sermon to him, starting him on his life-work. I feel as if I were Samuel at Bethlehem, seeking for David, to anoint him with a horn of oil in the name of the Lord. Some beloved people are here who have done a good deal, and the Lord has blessed them; but their work is heavy and their hearts are weary. By the anointing which has given you the kingdom, I trust that you will not be weary in well-doing. Pluck up courage, for a grand future is before you. "Who knows whether you are come to the kingdom for such a time as this?" Be content to be a living sacrifice. Say with Esther, "If I perish, I perish. I am content to give myself up for such a cause. Come life, come death, I am all His own; if I die in my Lord's work, I die content."

Further, "Who knows whether you are come to the kingdom for such a time as this?" *You do not yourself know.* I speak experimentally, using my own self as an instance in the work which God has enabled me to do. If it had been revealed to me that I should have enjoyed the opportunities which have fallen to my lot, I could never have believed it. If the Lord could use *me*, He can also use *you*. Only stand in a waiting posture, saying, "Here am I, send me!" and you will see things which you dare not expect. If the curtain could be opened, and you could behold the future, you would exclaim, "Is your servant born of angels that he should attempt such things as these?" I do not suppose Peter, James, and John had any inkling of what the Lord was going to do by them when they left their boats and nets at His call. John dreamed that one day he might sit on one earthly throne and his brother James on another, but this was not to be: yet have they obtained a nobler heritage. To each of us there is a share in the purposes of heaven, and this is a kingdom large enough. Who knows, brother or sister, whether you are put in your family to save it? Who knows whether you are made to live in a back street to bless that street? Who knows whether you are set down in a forlorn district to upraise that district? Who knows whether you are put into that nation to save that nation? Ay, put into the world in Christ's name to save the world? Aspire to great things for God. IV. Our fourth word is—

Confide

"Who knows whether you are come to the kingdom for such a time as this?" If you are come to the kingdom for such a time as this, *be confident that you are safe.* If God has brought Esther to the throne that she may go in unto the king and save her people; go in, good Esther! Fear not! Fast and pray your three days before you go; but be not dismayed. If the womanhood in you trembles in the prospect of a possible death, let confidence in God override your fears. Ahasuerus cannot kill you; you cannot die: he can refuse his golden scepter to all the princes of the empire, but not to you; for God has placed you where you are, and ordained you for His purpose. Rest assured if He had meant to destroy you He would not have shown you such things as these. Fall back on His past mercy and be confident.

What is more, if God has a purpose to serve by a certain person that person will live out his day and *accomplish the divine design.* The more resistance he experiences the more surely will his life-work be achieved. If all the devils in hell rose up at once against a true, devoted servant of God, who has a work to do, in the name of the Lord he would drive them away as smoke before the wind. David said, "They compass me about like bees, yea, they compass me about; but in the name of the Lord will I destroy them."

It is a bad day for anybody when he opposes himself to the manifest destiny of one of the Lord's commissioned ones. I fall back often on the grand truth of predestination: it is no sleepy doctrine to me. If God so decrees there is no altering it, and if He has purposed it there is no defeating it. Heaven and earth shall sooner fail than the eternal purpose.

Each servant of God is like the word which called him: as the word of the Lord does not return unto Him void, but prospers in the thing whereto He sent it, even so shall it be with every servant of the Most High. A holy confidence in the divine purpose instead of making men grow stolid and idle may prove to be one of the mightiest impulses to the heroic life. Cromwell's Ironsides to a man believed in the everlasting purpose, therefore they were invincible, for no fear ever breathed upon them. Though the hosts of the tyrant may be innumerable, yet with the war cry, "The Lord of hosts is with us," we will ride forth conquering and to conquer.

Settle it in your mind that the Lord has called you to the work, and then advance without question or fear. Put your hand to the plow, and pause not. Do the work with your might. Do not stand asking how: do it as you can. Do not stand asking when; do it directly. Do not say, "But I am weak"—the Lord is strong. Do not say, "But I must devise methods." Do not concoct schemes or tarry to perfect your methods: fling yourself upon the work with all your might.

Load your cannon with rough bits of rock or stones from the road if nothing better comes to hand; ram them in with plenty of powder; and apply the fire. When you have nothing else to hurl at the foe, place yourself in the gun. Believe me, no shot will be more effectual than hurling of your whole being into the conflict.

There was a man who strove in the House of Commons for what he thought would be a great boon to seamen, but he could not prevail. At last he broke through all the rules of the house and acted like a fanatic, and when everybody saw that the man was so in earnest that he was ready to faint and die, they said, "We must do something"; and it was done.

An enthusiasm which overpowers yourself is likely to overpower others. Do not fail for lack of fervor. Never mind if men think you crazy. When you are overwhelmed yourself the flood of zeal will bear all opposition before it. When you become so fanatically insane as to be absorbed by a passion for the glory of God, the salvation of men, the spread of truth, and the reclaiming of the fallen masses, there shall be about you the truest sanity, and the mightiest force.

May you feel such a passion concerning missions today. May you feel that the gospel must be preached to all nations. May you feel that impulse at this moment while we worship God by giving our contributions to His cause.

2

*The Good Shepherdess**

Tell me, O thou whom my soul loveth, where thou feedest, where
thou makest thy flock to rest at noon: for why should I be as one that
turneth aside by the flocks of thy companions? If thou know not, O
thou fairest among women, go thy way forth by the footsteps of the
flock, and feed thy kids beside the shepherds' tents (Song of
Solomon 1:7–8).

The bride was most unhappy and ashamed because her personal
beauty had been sorely marred by the heat of the sun. The fairest
among women had become swarthy as a sunburnt slave. Spiritually
it is so full often with a chosen soul. The Lord's grace has made her fair to
look upon, even as the lily; but she has been so busy about earthly things
that the sun of worldliness has injured her beauty. The bride with holy
shamefacedness exclaims, "Look not upon me, for I am black, because the
sun hath looked upon me." She dreads alike the curiosity, the admiration,
the pity, and the scorn of men, and turns herself alone to her Beloved,
whose gaze she knows to be so full of love that her swarthiness will not
cause her pain when most beneath His eye. This is one index of a gracious
soul—that whereas the ungodly rush to and fro, and know not where to
look for consolation, the believing heart naturally flies to its Well-beloved
Savior, knowing that in Him is its only rest.

It would appear from the preceding verse that the bride was also in trouble about a certain charge which had been given to her, which burdened
her, and in the discharge of which she had become negligent of herself. She
says, "They made me the keeper of the vineyards," and she would wish to
have kept them well, but she felt she had not done so, and that, moreover,
she had failed in a more immediate duty—"Mine own vineyard have I not
kept." Under this sense of double unworthiness and failure, feeling her
omissions and her commissions to be weighing her down, she turned round

* This sermon is taken from *The Metropolitan Tabernacle Pulpit* and was
preached on Sunday morning, June 1, 1873.

19

to her Beloved and asked instruction at His hands. This was well. Had she not loved her Lord she would have shunned Him when her comeliness was faded, but the instincts of her affectionate heart suggested to her that He would not discard her because of her imperfections. She was, moreover, wise thus to appeal to her Lord against herself. Beloved, never let sin part you from Jesus. Do not fly from Him under a sense of sin; that were foolishness. Sin may drive you *from* Sinai; it ought to draw you *to* Calvary. To the fountain we should fly with all the greater alacrity when we feel that we are foul; and to the dear wounds of Jesus, whence all our life and healing must come, we should resort with the greater earnestness when we feel our soul to be sick, even though we fear that sickness to be unto death. In the case, the bride takes her troubles, her distress about herself, and her confession concerning her work to Jesus. She brings before Him her double charge, the keeping of her own vineyard, and the keeping of the vineyards of others.

I know that I am speaking to many this morning who are busy in serving their Lord; and it may be that they feel great anxiety because they cannot keep their own hearts near to Jesus: they do not feel themselves warm and lively in the divine service; they plod on, but they are very much in the condition of those who are described as "faint, yet pursuing." When Jesus is present labor for Him is joy, but in His absence His servants feel like workers underground, bereft of the light of the sun. They cannot give up working for Jesus; they love Him too well for that, but they pine to have His company while they are working for Him, and like the young prophets who went to the wood to cut down every man a beam for their new house, they say to their master, "Be content, we pray you, and go with your servants." Our most earnest desire is that we may enjoy sweet communion with Jesus while we are actively engaged in His cause. Indeed, beloved, this is most important to all of us. I do not know of any point which Christian workers need more often to think upon than the subject of keeping their work and themselves near to the master's hand.

Our text will help us to this, under three heads. We have here, first, *a question asked*: "Tell me, O thou whom my soul loveth, where thou feedest, where thou makest thy flock to rest at noon?" Secondly, *an argument used*: "Why should I be as one that turneth aside by the flocks of thy companions?" And, thirdly, we have *an answer obtained*: "If thou know not, O thou fairest among women, go thy way forth by the footsteps of the flock, and feed thy kids beside the shepherds' tents." I. Here is

A Question Asked

Every word of the inquiry is worthy of our careful meditation. You will observe, first, concerning it, that it is *asked in love*. She calls Him to whom she speaks by the endearing title, "O thou whom my soul loveth."

Whatever she may feel herself to be, she knows that she loves *Him*. She is black, and ashamed to have her face gazed upon, but still she loves her Bridegroom. She has not kept her own vineyard as she ought to have done, but still she loves Him; that she is sure of, and therefore boldly declares it. She loves Him as she loves none other in all the world. He only can be called "Him whom my soul loveth." She knows none at all worthy to be compared with Him, none who can rival Him. He is her Lord, the sole prince and monarch of all her affections. She feels also that she loves Him intensely—from her inmost *soul* she loves Him. The life of her existence is bound up with Him: if there be any force and power and vitality in her, it is but as fuel to the great flame of her love, which burns alone for Him.

Mark well that it is not "O thou whom my soul believes in." That would be true but she has passed further. It is not "O thou whom my soul honors." That is true too, but she has passed beyond that stage. Nor is it merely "O thou whom my soul trusts and obeys." She is doing that, but she has reached something warmer, more tender, more full of fire and enthusiasm and it is "O thou whom my soul *loveth*."

Now, beloved, I trust many of us can speak so to Jesus. He is to us the Well-beloved, "the chief among a myriad": "His mouth is every sweetness, yea, all of Him is loveliness," and our soul is enraptured by Him, our heart is altogether taken up with Him. We shall never serve Him aright unless it be so. Before our Lord said to Peter, "Feed my lambs," and "Feed my sheep," He put the question, "Simon, son of Jonas, lovest thou me?" and this He repeated three times; for until that question is settled we are unfit for His service. So the bride here, having both herself and her little flock to care for, avows that she loves the spouse as if she felt that she would not dare to have a part of His flock to look after if she did not love Himself; as if she saw that her right to be a shepherdess at all depended upon her love *to* the Great Shepherd.

She could not expect His help in her work, much less His fellowship in the work, unless there was first in her that all-essential fitness of love to His person. The question therefore becomes instructive to us, because it is addressed to Christ under a most endearing title; and I ask every worker here to take care that He always does His work in a spirit of love, and always regards the Lord Jesus not as a task-master, not as one who has given us work to do from which we wish to escape, but as our dear Lord, whom to serve is bliss, and for whom to die is gain. "O thou whom my soul loveth," is the right name by which a worker for Jesus should address his Lord.

Now note that the question, as it is asked in love, is also *asked of Him*. "Tell me, O thou whom my soul loveth, where thou feedest." She asked Him to tell her, as if she feared that none but Himself would give her the correct answer; others might be mistaken, but He could not be. She asked of Him because she was quite sure that He would give her the kindest answer. Others might be indifferent, and might scarcely take the trouble to reply: but if Jesus would tell her Himself, with His own lips, He would mingle love with every word, and so console as well as instruct her. Perhaps she felt that nobody else could tell her as He could, for others speak to the ear, but He speaks to the heart: others speak with lower degrees of influence, we hear their speech but are not moved thereby; but Jesus speaks, and the Spirit goes with every word He utters, and therefore we hear to profit when He converses with us.

I do not know how it may be with you this morning, but I feel that if I could get half a word from Christ it would satisfy my soul for many a day. I love to hear the gospel, and to read it, and to preach it; but to hear it fresh from Himself, applied by the energy of the Holy Spirit! O this were refreshment! This were energy and power! Therefore, Savior, when Your workers desire to know where You feed, tell them Yourself, speak to their hearts by Your own Spirit and let them feel as though it were a new revelation to their inmost nature. "Tell me, O thou whom my soul loveth." It is asked in love: it is asked of Him.

Now, observe what the question is. She wishes to know how Jesus does His work, and where He does it. It appears, from the eighth verse, that she herself has a flock of sheep to tend. She is a shepherdess, and desires to feed her flock; hence her question, "Tell me where thou feedest?" She desires those little ones of hers to obtain rest as well as food, and she is troubled about them; therefore she says, "Tell me where thou makest thy flock to rest," for if she can see how Jesus does His work, and where He does it, and in what way, then she will be satisfied that she is doing it in the right way, if she closely imitates Him and abides in fellowship with Him. The question seems to be just this: "Lord, tell me what are the truths which You feed Your people's souls; tell me what are the doctrines which make the strong ones weak and the sad ones glad: tell me what is that precious meat which You give to hungry and fainting spirits, to revive them and keep them alive; for if You tell me, then I will give my flock the same food. Tell me where the pasture is wherein You feed Your sheep, and straightway I will lead mine to the self-same happy fields. Then tell me how You make Your people to rest. What are those promises which You apply to the consolation of their spirit, so that their cares and doubts and fears and agitations all subside?

You have sweet meadows where You make Your beloved flock to lie calmly down and slumber, tell me where those meadows are that I may go and fetch the flock committed to my charge, the mourners whom I ought to comfort, the distressed ones whom I am bound to relieve, the desponding whom I have endeavored to encourage; tell me, Lord, where You make Your flock to lie down, for then, under Your help, I will go and make my flock to lie down too. It is for myself, but yet far more for others, that I ask the question, 'Tell me where You feed, where You make them to rest at noon.'" I have no doubt that the spouse did desire information for herself and for her own good, and I believe Dr. Watts had caught some of the spirit of the passage when he sang—

> Fain would I feed among Thy sheep,
> Among them rest, among them sleep.

But it does not strike me that this is all the meaning of the passage by a very long way. The bride says, "Tell me where you feed Your flock," as if she would wish to feed with the flock; "where you make Your flock to rest," as if she wanted to rest there too: but it strikes me the very gist of the thing is this, that she wished to bring her flock to feed where Christ's flock feeds, and to lead her kids to lie down where Christ's little lambs were reposing; she desired, in fact, to do her work in His company; she wanted to mix up her flock with the Lord's flock, her work with His work, and to feel that what she was doing she was doing for Him, yea, and with Him and through Him. She had evidently met with a great many difficulties in what she had tried to do. She wished to feed her flock of kids, but could not find them pasture.

Perhaps when she began her work as a shepherdess she thought herself quite equal to the task, but now the same sun which had bronzed her face had dried up the pasture, and so she says, "O You who know all the pastures, tell me where You feed, for I cannot find grass for my flock"; and suffering herself from the noontide head, she finds her little flock suffering too; and she inquires "Where do You make Your flock to rest at noon? Where are cool shadows of great rocks which screen off the sultry rays when the sun is in its zenith and pours down torrents of heat? For I cannot shade my poor flock and give them comfort in their many trials and troubles. I wish I could. O Lord, tell me the secret of Your consolation; then will I try to console my own charge by the self-same means." We would know the groves of promise and the cool streams of peace, that we may lead others into rest. If we can follow Jesus we can guide others, and so both we and they will find comfort and peace. That is the meaning of the request before us.

Note well that she said most particularly, "Tell *me*." "O Master, do not merely tell our sheep where You feed, though they want to know; but tell me where You feed, for I would gladly instruct others." She would know many things, but chiefly she says, "Tell me *where You feed*," for she wished to feed others. We want practical knowledge, for our desire is to be helped to bring others into rest; to be the means of speaking peace to the consciences of others, as the Lord has spoken peace to ours. Therefore the prayer is, "Tell me." "You are my model, O Great Shepherd; You are my wisdom. If I be a shepherd to Your sheep, yet am I also a sheep beneath Your Shepherdry, therefore teach me, that I may teach others."

I do not know whether I make myself plain to you, but I wish to put it very simply. I am preaching to myself perhaps a great deal more than to you. I am preaching to my own heart. I feel I have to come, Sunday after Sunday, and weekday after weekday, and tell you a great many precious things about Christ, and sometimes I enjoy them myself; and if nobody else gets blessed by them, I do, and I go home and praise the Lord for it; but my daily fear is lest I should be a handler of texts for you, and a preacher of good things for others, and yet remain unprofited in my own heart. My prayer is that the Lord Jesus will show me where He feeds His people, and let me feed with them, that then I may conduct you to the pastures where He is, and be with Him myself at the same time that I bring you to Him.

You Sunday school teachers and evangelists, and others, my dear, earnest comrades, for whom I thank God at every remembrance, I feel that the main point you have to watch about is that you do not lose your own spirituality while trying to make others spiritual. The great point is to live near to God. It would be a dreadful thing for you to be very busy about other men's souls and neglect your own. Appeal to the Well-beloved, and entreat Him to let you feed your flock where He is feeding His people, that He would let you sit at His feet, like Mary, even while you are working in the house, like Martha. Do not do less, but rather more; but ask to do it in such communion with Him that your work will be melted into His work, and what you are doing will be really only His working in you, and you rejoicing to pour out to others what He pours into your own soul. God grant it may be so with you all, beloved. II. Secondly, here is

An Argument Used

The bride says, "Why should I be as one who turns aside by the flocks of Your companions?" If she should lead her flock into distant meadows, far away from the place where Jesus is feeding His flock, it would not be well. As a shepherdess would naturally be rather dependent, and would need to associate herself for protection with others, suppose she should turn aside with other shepherds, and leave her Bridegroom, would it be right? She speaks of it as a thing most abhorrent to her mind, and well might it be. For, first, would it not look very unseemly that the bride should be associating with others than the Bridegroom? They have each a flock: there is He with His great flock, and here is she with her little one. Shall they seek pastures far off from one another? Will there not be talk about this? Will not onlookers say, "This is not seemly: there must be some lack of love here, or else these two would not be so divided"?

Stress may be put, if you like, upon that little word "I." Why should *I*, your blood-bought spouse; I, betrothed unto You, or ever the earth was, I, whom You have loved—why should I turn after others and forget thee? Beloved, you had better put the emphasis in your own reading of it just there. Why should *I*, whom the Lord has pardoned the Lord has loved, whom the Lord has favored so much—I, who have enjoyed fellowship with Him for many years—I, who know that His love is better than wine—I, who have aforetime been inebriated with His sweetness—Why should I turn aside? Let others do so if they will, but it would be uncomely and unseemly for me.

I pray you, brothers and sisters, try to feel that—that for you to work apart from Christ would have a bad look about it; that for your work to take you away from fellowship with Jesus would have a very ugly appearance: it would not be among the things that are honest and of good repute. For the bride to feed her flock in other company would look like unfaithfulness to her husband.

What, shall the bride of Christ forsake her Beloved? Shall she be unchaste toward her Lord? Yet it would seem so if she makes companions of others and forgets her Beloved! Our hearts may grow unchaste to Christ even while they are zealous in Christian work. I dread very much the tendency to do Christ's work in a cold, mechanical spirit; but above even that I tremble lest I should be able to have warmth for Christ's work and yet should be cold toward the Lord Himself. I fear that such a condition of heart is possible—that we may burn great bonfires in the streets for public display, and scarcely keep a live coal upon our hearth for Jesus to warm His hands at.

When we meet in the great assembly the good company helps to warm our hearts, and when we are working for the Lord with others they stimulate us and cause us to put forth all our energy and strength, and then we think, "Surely my heart is in a healthy condition toward God." But, beloved, such excitement may be a poor index of our real state. I love that quiet, holy fire which will glow in the closet and flame forth in the chamber when I am alone, and that is the point I am more fearful about than anything else, both for myself and for you, lest we should be doing Christ's work without Christ; having much to do but not thinking much of *Him*; cumbered about much serving and forgetting Him. Why, that would soon grow into making a Christ out of our own service, an Antichrist out of our own labors. Beware of that! Love your work, but love your Master better; love your flock, but love the great Shepherd better still, and ever keep close to Him, for it will be a token of unfaithfulness if you do not.

And mark again, "Why should I be as one who turns aside by the flocks of Your companions?" We may read this as meaning, "Why should I be so unhappy as to have to work for You, and yet be out of communion with You?" It is an unhappy thing to lose fellowship with Jesus, and yet to have to go on with religious exercises. If the wheels are taken off your chariot, it is no great matter if nobody wants to ride, but how if you are called upon to drive on? When a man's foot is lamed he may not so much regret it if he can sit still, but if he be bound to run a race he is greatly to be pitied. It made the spouse doubly unhappy even to suppose that she, with her flock to feed and herself needing feeding too, should have to turn aside by the flocks of others and miss the presence of her Lord. In fact, the question seems to be put in this shape: "What reason is there why I should leave my Lord? What apology could I make, what excuse could I offer for so doing? Is there any reason why I should not abide in constant fellowship with Him? Why should I be as one who turns aside?

Perhaps it may be said that others turn aside, but why should *I* be as one of them? There may be excuses for such an act in others, but there can be none for me: Your rich love, O Lord, Your free love, Your undeserved love, Your special love to me, has bound me hand and foot: how can I turn aside? There may be some professors who owe You little, but I, once the chief of sinners, owe You so much, how can I turn aside? There may be some with whom You have dealt hardly who may turn aside, but You have been so tender, so kind to me, how can I forget You? There may be some who know but little of You, whose experience of You is so slender that their turning aside is not to be wondered at; but how can I turn aside when You have showed me Your love, and revealed Your heart to me? Oh, by the banqueting house where I have feasted with You, by the Hermonites and the hill Mizar, where You have manifested Your love, by the place where deep called to deep, and then mercy called to mercy; by those mighty storms and sweeping hurricanes in which You were the shelter of my head, by ten thousand thousand mercies past which have been my blessed portion, why should *I* be as one who turns aside by the flocks of Your companions?"

Let me address the members of this church, and say to you, if all the churches in Christendom were to go aside from the gospel, why should you? If in every other place the gospel should be neglected, and an uncertain sound should be given forth; if Ritualism should swallow up half the churches, and Rationalism the rest, yet why should *you* turn aside? You have been peculiarly a people of prayer; you have also followed the Lord fully in doctrine and in ordinance; and consequently you have enjoyed the divine presence, and have prospered beyond measure. We have cast ourselves upon the Holy Spirit for strength, and have not relied upon human eloquence, music, or beauties of color, or architecture. Our only weapon has been the simple, plain, full gospel, and why should we turn aside? Have we not been favored for these many years with unsurpassed success? Has not the Lord added unto our numbers so abundantly that we have not had room enough to receive them? Has He not multiplied the people, and increased the joy? Hold fast to your first love, and let no man take your crown. I thank God there are churches still, a few in England and yet more in Scotland, which hold fast the doctrines of the gospel and will not let them go. To them I would say, why should you turn aside? Should not your history, both in its troublous and its joyous chapters, teach you to hold fast the form of sound words?

Above all, should we not try to live as a church, and individually, also, in abiding fellowship with Jesus; for if we turn aside from Him we shall rob the truth of its aroma, yea, of its essential fragrance. If we lose fellowship with Jesus we shall have the standard, but where will be the standard-bearer? We may retain the candlestick, but where shall be the light? We shall be shorn of our strength, our joy, our comfort, our all, if we miss fellowship with Him. God grant, therefore, that we may never be as those who turn aside.

An Answer Given

III. Thirdly, we have here AN ANSWER GIVEN by the Bridegroom to His beloved. She asked Him where He fed, where He made His flock to rest, and He answered her. Observe carefully that this answer is *given in tenderness to her infirmity*; not ignoring her ignorance, but dealing very gently with it. "If you know not"—a hint that she ought to have known, but such a hint as kind lovers give when they would forbear to chide. Our Lord is very tender to our ignorance. There are many things which we do not know, but ought to have known. We are children when we should be men, and have to be spoken to as unto carnal—unto babes in Christ, when we should have become fathers. Is there one among us who can say, "I am not faulty in my knowledge"? I am afraid the most of us confess that if we had done the Lord's will better we should have known His doctrine better; if we had lived more closely to Him we should have known more of Him. Still, how very gentle the rebuke is. The Lord forgives our ignorance, and condescends to instruct it.

Note next that the answer is *given in great love*. He says, "O fairest among women." That is a blessed cordial for her distress. She said, "I am black"; but He says, "O fairest among women." I would rather trust Christ's eyes than mine. If my eyes tell me I am black I will weep, but if He assures me I am fair I will believe Him and rejoice. Some saints are more apt to remember their sinfulness, and grieve over it, than to believe in their righteousness in Christ, and triumph in it. Remember, beloved, it is quite as true today that you are all fair and without spot as you are black, because the sun has looked upon you. It must be true, because Jesus says so. Let me give you one of the sayings of the Bridegroom to His bride: "You are all fair, my love; there is no spot in you." "Ah, that is a figure," you say. Well, I will give you one that is not a figure. The Lord Jesus, after He had washed His disciples' feet, said, "He who is washed need not wash his feet for he is clean every whit"; and then He added, "And you are clean." If you desire an apostolic word to the same effect, let me give you this: "Who shall lay anything to the charge of God's elect?"—*anything*—

any little thing or any great thing either. Jesus has washed His people so clean that there is no spot, no wrinkle, nor any such thing upon them in the matter of justification before God.

> In thy Surety thou art free,
> His dear hands were pierced for thee;
> With His spotless vesture on,
> Holy as the Holy One.

How glorious this is. Jesus does not exaggerate when He thus commends His church. He speaks plain, sober truth: "O thou fairest among women." My soul, do you not feel love to Christ when you remember that He thinks you are beautiful? I cannot see anything in myself to love, but He does, calls me "all fair." I think it must be that He looks into our eyes and sees, Himself, or else this, that He know what we are going to be, and judges us on that scale. As the artist, looking on the block of marble, sees in the stone the statue which he means to etch out of it with matchless skill, so the Lord Jesus sees the perfect image of Himself in us, from which He means to chip away the imperfections and the sins until it stands out in all its splendor. But still it is gracious condescension which makes Him say, "You are the fairest among women," to one who mourned her own sunburnt countenance.

The answer contains much sacred wisdom. The bride is directed where to go that she may find her beloved and lead her flock to Him. "Go thy way forth by the footprints of the flock." If you will find Jesus, you will find Him in the way the holy prophets went, in the way of the patriarchs and the way of the apostles. And if you desire to find your flock, and to make them lie down, very well, go and feed them as other shepherds have done—Christ's own shepherds whom He has sent in other days to feed His chosen.

I feel very glad, in speaking from this text, that the Lord does not give to His bride in answer to her question some singular directions of great difficulty, some novel prescriptions singular and remarkable. Just as the Gospel itself is simple and homely, so is this exhortation and direction for the renewal of communion. It is easy, it is plain. You want to get to Jesus, and you want to bring those under your charge to Him. Very well, then, do not seek out a new road, but simply go the way which all other saints have gone. If you want to walk with Jesus, walk where other saints have walked; and if you want to lead others in communion with Him, lead them by your example where others have gone.

What is that? If you want to be with Jesus, go where Abraham when in the path of separation. See how He lived as a pilgrim and a sojourner with His God. If you would see Jesus, "Come out from among them, be . . . separate, touch not the unclean thing." You shall find Jesus when you have left the world. If you would walk with Jesus, follow the path of obedience. Saints have never had fellowship with Jesus when they have disobeyed Him. Keep

His statutes and observe His testimonies, be jealous over your conduct and character; for the path of obedience is the path of communion. Be sure that you follow the ancient ways with regard to the Christ ordinances: do not alter them, but keep to the good old paths. Stand and inquire what apostles did, and do the same. Jesus will not bless you in using fanciful ceremonies of human invention. Keep to those which He commands, which His Spirit sanctions, and which His apostles practiced. Above all, if you would walk with Jesus, continue in the way of holiness; persevere in the way of grace. Make the Lord Jesus your model and example; and by treading where the footprints of the flock are to be seen, you will both save yourself and them who hear you; you will find Jesus, and they will find Jesus too.

We might have supposed that the Lord would have said, "If you want to lead your flock aright, array yourself in sumptuous apparel, or go get your music and fine anthems; by these fair things you will fascinate the Savior into your sanctuaries": but it is not so. The incense which will please the Lord Jesus is that of holy prayer and praise, and the only Ritualism which is acceptable with Him is this—pure religion, and undefiled before God and the Father. It is this, to visit the fatherless and the widow, and to keep oneself unspotted from the world. This is all He wants. Follow that, and you shall both go right, and lead others right.

Then the Spouse added, "Feed thy kids beside the shepherds' tents." Now, who are these shepherds? There are many in these days who set up for shepherds, who feed their sheep in poisonous pastures. Keep away from them; but there are others whom it is safe to follow. Let me take you to the twelve principal shepherds who came after the great Shepherd of all. You want to bless your children, to save their souls, and have fellowship with Christ in the doing of it; then teach them the truths which the apostles taught. And what were they?

Take Paul as an example. "I determined not to know anything among you save Jesus Christ, and him crucified." That is feeding the kids beside the shepherds' tents, when you teach your children Christ, much of Christ, all of Christ, and nothing else but Christ. Mind you stick to that blessed subject. And when you are teaching them Christ, teach them all about His life, His death, His resurrection; teach them His Godhead and His manhood. You will never enjoy Christ's company if you doubt His divinity.

Take care that you feed your flock upon the doctrine of the atonement. Christ will have no fellowship with a worker unless he represents Him fairly, and you cannot represent Christ truthfully unless you see the ruddy hue of His atoning blood as well as the lily purity of His life. "Feed thy kids beside the shepherds' tents," then will you teach them the atoning sacrifice, and justification by faith, and imputed righteousness, and union with the risen Head, and the coming of the great One, wherein we shall receive the adoption, to wit, the redemption of the body from the grave.

I speak the truth and lie not when I say that if we want to teach a congregation so as to bless them, and keep in fellowship with Christ at the same time ourselves, we must be very particular to teach nothing but the truth—not a part of it, but all of it. Preach that blessed doctrine of *election*. Oh, the deeps of divine love which are contained in that blessed truth! Do not shirk it, or keep it in the background. You cannot expect Christ's presence if you do. Teach the doctrine of *man's depravity*. Lay the sinner low. God will not bless a ministry which exalts men. Preach the doctrine of *the Holy Spirit's effectual calling*, for if we do not magnify the Spirit of God, we cannot expect that He will make our work to stand. Preach *regeneration*. Let it be seen how thorough the change is, that we may glorify God's work.

Preach the *final perseverance of the saints*. Teach that the Lord is *not changeable*—casting away His people, loving them today and hating them tomorrow. Preach, in fact, the doctrines of *grace* as you find them in the Book. Feed them beside the shepherds' tents. Ay, and feed the kids there— the little children. I begin to feel more and more that it is a mistake to divide the children from the congregation. I believe in special services for children, but I would also have them worship with us. If our preaching does not teach children, it lacks some element which it ought to possess. The kind of preaching which is best of all for grown-up people is that in which children also will take delight. I like to see the congregation made up not all of the young, nor all of the old; not all of the mature, nor all of the inexperienced, but some of all sorts gathered together.

If we are teaching children salvation by works, and grown-up people salvation by grace, we are pulling down in the school-room what we build up in the church, and that will never do. Feed the kids with the same gospel as the grown-up sheep, though not exactly in the same terms; let your language be appropriate to them, but let it be the same truth. God forbid that we should have our Sunday schools the hot-beds of Arminianism, while our churches are gardens of Calvinism. We shall soon have a division in the camp if that be so.

The same truth for all; and you cannot expect Christ to be with you in feeding your little flocks unless you feed them where Christ feeds us. Where does He feed us but where the truth grows? Oh, when I read some sermons, they remind me of a piece of common by the roadside, after a hungry horde of sheep have devoured every green thing; but when I read a solid gospel sermon of the Puritans, it reminds me of a field kept for hay, which a farmer is at last obliged to give up to the sheep. The grass has grown almost as high as themselves, and so they lie down in it, eating and resting too.

Give me the doctrines of grace, and I am in clover. If you have to feed others, take them there. Do not conduct them to the starved pastures of modern thought and culture. Preachers are starving God's people nowadays, Oh, but they set out such beautiful China plates, such wonderful knives and forks, such marvelous vases and damask tablecloths! But as for food, the plates look as if they had been smeared with a feather, there is so little on them. The real gospel teaching is little enough. They give us nothing to learn, nothing to digest, nothing to feed upon; it is all slops, and nothing substantial.

O for the good old corn of the kingdom; we want that, and I am persuaded that when the churches get back to the old food again, when they begin to feed their flocks beside the shepherds' tents, and when in practical living, Christians, the saints, get back to the old Puritanic method, and follow once again the tracks of the sheep, and the sheep follow the tracks of Christ, then we shall get the church into fellowship with Jesus, and Jesus will do wonders in our midst. But to get that, each individual must aim at winning it for himself; and if the Lord shall grant it to each one of us, then it will be granted to the whole, and the good times which we desire will certainly have come.

Beloved, do you desire to work with Christ? Do you want to feel that Jesus is at your right hand? Then go and work in His way. Teach what He would have you teach, not what you would like to teach. Go and work for Him, as He would have you work, not as your prejudices might prescribe to you. Be obedient. Follow the footsteps of the flock. Be diligent also to keep close to the shepherds' tents, and the Lord bless you more and more, you and your children, and His shall be the glory.

I have spoken only to God's people: I would there had been time to speak to the unconverted too, but to them I can only say this: may God grant you grace to know the beauties of Jesus, for then you will love Him too. May He also show you the deformities of yourselves, for then you will desire to be cleansed and made lovely in Christ.

And remember, if any one of you wants Christ, *He* wants *you*; and if you long for Him, He longs for you. If you seek Him, He is seeking you. If you will not cry to Him, He is already crying after you. "Whosoever will, let Him come and take of the water of life freely." The Lord save you for His name's sake. Amen.

3

*Hagar: A Welcome Discovery**

God opened her eyes, and she saw a well of water; and she went and filled the bottle with water, and gave the lad drink (Genesis 21:19).

You know the story of Hagar; of her being sent out from Abraham's tent with her son Ishmael. It was necessary that they should be sent away from the child of promise. God, nevertheless, had designs of good toward Ishmael and his mother. Still he tried them. Whether we be saints or sinners, we shall meet with tribulation. Whether it is Sarah or Hagar, no life shall be without its affliction. To Hagar the affliction came in a very painful manner, for the little water that she had brought with her in her bottle was gone. She must give her child drink, or he would die, and then she by-and-by must follow. She laid the boy down, giving him up in despair, and began to weep what she thought would be her last flood of tears.

Still there was no real cause for her distress. She need not have thirsted; she was close by a well. In her grief she had failed to see it. The distraction of her spirit had made her look everywhere except to one place, where she would have found exactly what she wanted. God therefore spoke to her by an angel; and after having done that He opened her eyes, and she saw a well of water, which, I suppose, had always been there. When she saw it, she went at once to it, filled her bottle, gave her child to drink, and all her sorrows were over. It seemed a very simple remedy for a very sad case.

It is but an illustration of what is often happening in human life. Men and women come into sore trouble, and yet if they could see all around them they need not be in trouble. They actually come to death's door in their own judgment, and yet there really is, if they understood all things, no cause for their distress. They will escape out of their present trial

---

* This sermon is taken from *The Metropolitan Tabernacle Pulpit* and was preached at the Metropolitan Tabernacle, Newington, July, 1873.

as soon as ever their eyes are opened, for they will see that God has made provision for their necessities, prepared comfort for their griefs, and made such a way of escape from their fears that they need by no means give way to despair.

I desire to speak to persons who are in trouble. There are three things I shall bring before them. The first is, that it often happens with seeking persons, and troubled persons, that, as in Hagar's case, *the supply of their necessities is close at hand*—the well is near. Secondly, it often happens that the supply is *as much there as if it had been provided for them and for them only*, as this well seemed to have been. And, thirdly, *no great exertion is needed to procure from the supply already made by God all that we want.* She filled her bottle with water—a joyful task to her; and she gave the lad drink. I. It often happens that when we are in trouble and distress

The Supply of Our Need, and the Consolation for Our Sorrow Are Very Near at Hand

There is a well close to us at our feet, if we could but see it. We miss it perhaps; yet that is not because it is far away, but because our eyes are not open. There is no necessity for God to make a well—that has been done. What is necessary is that He should open our eyes, that we may see what is there already.

How true this often is in providence with Christian people. We have known them to be deeply concerned at some approaching ill, or in the most fearful distress on account of some troublous circumstances which already surround them. They have said, "We don't know what we shall do tomorrow." They have inquired, "Who shall roll us away the stone?" They know not that God has already provided for tomorrow, and has rolled the stone away. If they knew all, they would understand that their trial is purely imaginary. They are making it by their unbelief. It has no other existence than that which their distrust of God gives to it. While they are inquiring, "Where shall I find a friend? Who will come to the rescue?" the friend is already in the house, or, perhaps, will never be wanted at all. While they are saying, "How can I get out of this dilemma?" God has already solved it; the riddle has been answered; the enigma has been explained. They are troubled about a difficulty which has already been disentangled by the divine hand.

We have known persons to be utterly surprised when God has delivered them. This proves that their faith was small. With calm trust there is quiet waiting. They might well have expected that He would do it. Among the surprises such persons have expressed has been this—that, after all, He should have delivered them by a means so simple. "How could it have happened," say they, "that I could not have thought of this? That I should actually have the boon I crave hard by me, and yet not perceive it—that I should be thirsty and crying out to God, in hope that perhaps He will rend the heavens, and send a shower of rain, and all the while there is the well bubbling up with fresh water." We have only got to look to find it, and having found it we have only to stoop down to take and to drink thereof for our refreshment.

Children of God; you who are troubled about providence, pray God to help you to trust when you cannot trace your God. Ask Him to give you, not what you wish for, but resignation to His wishes; ask to have His will casting its shadow over your soul, and let that shadow be your will henceforth. O that we had learned, in whatsoever state we are, therewith to be content, basing our confidence on this sure promise—He has said, "I will never leave you nor forsake you." This is the best foundation for contentment that will ever be found. O for grace to feel that if we cannot tell how God will deliver us, it is no business of ours to be able to tell; that if God knows, that is enough. God has not set us to be the providers; He does not intend us to hold the helm, and to pull the leading-strings. 'Tis ours to follow, not to lead; 'tis ours to obey, and not to prescribe for God. Your deliverance is near, O child of sorrow; or if it tarry for awhile, it shall be but the richer blessing when it comes. Ships that are long upon the sea are, perhaps, the more heavily freighted; and when they do come to the port, they will bring home a double cargo of blessing. Those plants that come up quickly when they are sown in the ground last but for a little while. Perhaps the blessing that is so long in springing out of the soil of your expectancy will last you all your life long. Therefore, if the vision tarry, wait for it with patience.

Though this is true of providence, I prefer rather to deal with the matter of spiritual blessings. It often happens that souls are disturbed in spiritual matters about things that ought not to disturb them. For instance, a large proportion of spiritual distresses are occasioned by a forgetfulness or an ignorance of the doctrines of the Bible.

We have met with young persons frequently who have made the astounding discovery that their hearts are desperately wicked. They were converted some time ago, and made a profession of their faith. They did then really repent of sin, and they laid hold on Christ, but their experience was comparatively superficial. After awhile the Holy Spirit was pleased to show them more of the hidden evils of their nature, and to permit the fountains of the great deep of their original depravity to be broken up, and they have been in perfect consternation, as though some strange thing had happened to them, and they have said, "Where is the comfort for this?"

Now, if they had known at first that our nature is hopelessly bad, and that the Scripture describes it as such, they would not have been surprised when they found that truth out. And had they understood that the work of the Spirit is not to improve our nature—that He never tried to do it, and never intends to do it, but that He leaves the old nature to die, to be buried with Christ, and gives us a new nature which comes into conflict with the old nature, and causes an eternal war and strife within the spirit—had they been acquainted with those truths when they found sin breaking loose in them, and felt the conflict within, they would have said, "This is just what I was told would happen; this is the experience of the children of God. This is what Paul speak so in the seventh chapter of the Epistle to the Romans, and I am, after all, in the same way as the saints of God." Forgetting this, they think there is no comfort for them in what seems to them to be the strangest of all human experiences, but which, indeed, is an experience common to the people of God. They are looking for the well of water, when that very doctrine they have forgotten would furnish them with the refreshment they stand in need of.

We meet with others whose trouble is about their perseverance. They believe they are the people of God, but they tremble lest they should fail to hold on and maintain the good profession. Their trials are so severe, and they feel their own weakness to be so extreme, may they not one day slip with their feet to a foul and final fall, and be utterly destroyed? Ah, if they understood what I feel sure is the indisputable truth of God, that "the righteous shall hold on his way, and he who has clean hands shall wax stronger," they would not have been troubled about that question, provided they could answer the other one—are they righteous? Do they belong to those made righteous in Christ? "I give unto my sheep them out of my hands." What a magnificent assurance of the safety of all the sheep of God!

If I be but one of them, may I not feel a perfect confidence that Christ, who cannot lie, will make good His word? There are, besides this, innumerable other promises to the same effect, and oftentimes a man distressed about that might relieve his anxieties at once by the knowledge that it is a perfectly unscriptural apprehension that is agitating him. We are all too prone to judge by our feelings rather than to take counsel at the fountain head and rely on the oracle of inspiration.

I knew an excellent Christian woman whose trouble was of a somewhat queer character, for she said she knew she loved the Savior, and I think all who knew her felt that she did; but though she knew she loved the Savior, she was afraid that the Savior did not love her; nor was it easy to comfort her about that. Now, truly, if she could have grasped the thought that, "*We love him because he first loved us*," the snare would have been broken. Had she perceived that all that is in us must be first put into us if it be of any good; that the grace of God prevents us (goes before us); that it is the root and origin of any good thing in us; that the everlasting and eternal love of God is the fountain out of which our love to God must flow—had she known that, she would not have been troubled on that head.

I wonder sometimes how those friends who do not receive what is commonly called Calvinistic doctrine manage to be comforted. I certainly never have any quarrel with those on the other side of the opinion, for if their tenets have any sweetness to them, I am delighted to hear that any have tasted it. I am always glad that everything in the world should be eaten up, and if anybody can find any food and comfort there, I am glad to hear it. I could not, and therefore I do not envy them. I would not wish to deprive them of any comfort they could find there, as I have never been able to find any myself. If I believed that my own final perseverance rested with myself—if I thought that I might have a love to God that sprang up because of my own will rather than as a work of grace—I do not know, but I might be driven to utter distraction.

Some persons need solid food, and must have it, or their health would fail. So the firm belief that salvation is of grace from first to last, and that where God begins a good work He will carry it on, is essential to my Christian existence, and therefore I cannot give it up. Those who can do without it, let them, but as for me, I cannot. I have not any comfort left me if any one shall prove that these things are not the truth of holy Scripture. They *are* the truth of Scripture, however, and let any who are distressed remember them. May God open their eyes to see them, and they need to be thirsty no more.

Sometimes, beloved, holy Scripture has its well near to the troubled heart, not so much in the form of doctrine, as in the form of promise. There was never a trouble yet in human experience among God's people, but what there was a promise to meet it. You have only to look long enough, and you shall find the counterfoil; you will discover that God has in His book that which exactly meets your case.

"Oh," said Christian, in Bunyan's *Pilgrim*, "what a thousand fools have I been to lie rotting in this stinking dungeon all these weeks, when I have a key in my bosom which, I am persuaded, would fit the locks of all the doors in Doubting Castle. Come, good brother, let us try it." And so Christian plucked up courage, and he found his key of promise, though it grated a little; and Bunyan says that one of the doors went, as he puts it in his old edition, "damnably hard." He did not know how to put it strong enough until he used that word. Yet the key did open every single door, and even the iron gate itself, the external gate of the castle, opened by the help of the key.

O dear hearts, some of you have laid, fretting and worrying yourselves about things which God has dealt with already in His own word. You have said, "Would God He would do that!" and He has done it. You have asked Him to give you something, and you have received it. I have used sometimes the simile of a man in the dark dying of hunger, and yet he is shut up in the pantry. There is the food all around him, if he could only put out his hand to take it. Did he know it to be there, and would he grasp it, there is just what he wants. I am persuaded, beloved, if you search the Scriptures well, there is not one child of God here who need despair of finding that the Master has opened a well of promise for him.

At other times the well appears in the form neither of a doctrine nor of a promise, but in the shape of an experience of someone else. Perhaps nothing more effectually comforts, under the blessing of God, than the discovery that some undoubtedly good man has passed through the same state of heart in which we are found. When we see the footsteps of the flock, we hope that we are in the Shepherd's path. Now, if you are in deep trouble, may I invite you to read Psalm 81. What a psalm that is—that prayer of David's. Was ever man so cast out from God's sight, and banished from all hope, as he? Yet there was no brighter saint in the olden times than the renowned sufferer.

If you have deep castings down of spirit, I would invite you to consort with Job. Read that book through. See how terrible are some of his utterances, yet who shall doubt that Job was not only saved from his sins and redeemed from all adversity, but that he holds a name among the most illustrious of those who by faith have overcome the world?

Turn, if you need other examples, to the sighs of king Hezekiah, or to the lamentations of Jeremiah the Prophet. Surely there you shall find your own case in some chapter or another. And if it be a matter of inward contention, read the Epistle to the Romans, especially that part where Paul, in wondrous paradox, describes himself as doing that evil which he would not, and not doing that good which he would, and yet that which he did, he did not allow—till he cries, "O wretched man that I am! who shall deliver me from the body of this death?" You would find, my dear Christian brother or sister, that instead of your present pinch and trial being a strange thing, you are only suffering what God's children have the most of them suffered. You imagine yourself to be sailing over unknown seas, when you are but following the ordinary track-way of the saints around that cape of storms which, when it is better known, will be to you a Cape of Good Hope. Be of good comfort; be of good cheer; for the experience of others may refresh thee, as well as the promises and the doctrines which abound in the word of God.

And, beloved, sometimes it pleases the Holy Spirit to open a well of living waters for us in the person, and work, and life, and sympathy, and love, of our Well-beloved, the Lord Jesus Christ. Often when I have found myself depressed in spirit, I have challenged my soul, as it were, with this question—"Why are you cast down? Did not Jesus feel this?" and the depression has vanished. The thought that Christ has sympathy in this particular trial is an inexpressibly sweet one. When the Holy Spirit brings it home to the soul, we can bless the Savior's name that He did not merely carry our sins, but that He carried our sorrows; that He was not merely a substitute, which is the greatest of all consolations, but a sympathizer, which is also inexpressibly delightful to us. Jesus suffers with you, O child of God—suffers in you. You are a member of His body, and therefore He endures in you. You are making up that which is behind of the sufferings of Christ for His body's sake, which is the church.

There is so much of suffering allotted to the entire mystical body of Christ, that there is some of it left behind as yet, and you will have your share of it. Be thankful when you hear it that it is a part of the suffering of the body of Christ. And, oh, to look into His face by faith, and to feel that He is not hard or pitiless, whatever others may be! To look into His face when we are distressed by reason of the wrongs of others and the dishonor done to Christ's church, and to feel that He knows it, notices it, and has sympathy with us in our sorrow over declining zeal, or over the worldliness of His people—why that nerves us with new strength.

Does Jesus feel what we feel? Does He sympathize in it? Are we bearing it for His sake? Then we will take the trouble with welcome, and be glad to bear it, that He may be honored thereby. Beloved, if you have forgotten your Lord—(and perhaps some of you may, during this week, have been forgetting Him—it is no unusual thing)—think of Him again, and you shall find a well of water close to you.

Besides, once more, our sorrows often arise from our not observing the Holy Spirit. He is in us, and He shall be with us forever. We are troubled about the little progress of the kingdom of God in the world, but if we believe in the Holy Spirit we shall soon get our courage back again. There is no reason why the simplest sermon, preached in the humblest place, should not at any time be the commencement of a great revival. There is no reason known to us why the simple preaching of Jesus Christ, on any one Sabbath day, should not prove to be the conversion of all the hearers, and, through the hearers, very speedily of an entire nation. We do not know as yet—we have none of us, probably, any notion of—the great power of the Spirit of God.

Some years ago there left this coast a convict vessel full of the lowest class of men that could be got together—convicts sent out for long periods of exile. On board that vessel was a surgeon superintendent who loved the Savior—who believed in the gospel and prayed mightily. He called the convicts together, stated to them that he had an intense desire for the good of their souls—that he intended during the time of their voyage that such and such rules for their good should be observed—that he particularly wished that they should all learn to read that they might be able to read the Scriptures—that he should hold meetings each day—that he should pray for them individually. Within a short time some convicts were converted to God.

There came a storm in which a companion vessel containing 200 men went to the bottom, and this alarmed and aroused the consciences of the ungodly on board the vessel, made them more susceptible to the gospel, and rendered the task of teaching them the gospel much more easy than it had been before. Of course, the terror was transient, and being but a natural shock, wore away.

Still, in the meanwhile, the good man had availed himself of the opportunity. There suddenly broke out in that vessel a divine work, and all over it might have been heard, at almost any hour of the day or night, hardened men, criminals exiled from their country, crying out, "What must we do to be saved?" When they landed there was not one man or child out of all on board who did not profess to have found the Savior, for the Spirit of God had wrought powerfully among them. They had become, before they reached their distant destination, instead of a nest of swearing beings, whose very talk was profanity, and whose breath was blasphemy, a church of the living God.

Such results were produced by the power of God's Spirit in answer to prayer. And if the Spirit of God were to come upon any one here, be he who he might, a like transformation would be wrought. Though he were the most abandoned character, though his infidelity might have entrenched itself, as he imagines, behind a thousand arguments, the Spirit of God would pull these down, convince him of sin, renew him and change his heart at once.

Oh, would to God the church could say, "I believe in the Holy Spirit," for today she is like Hagar in the wilderness crying, and the angel says, "What ails you, Hagar?" and she says, "I want more ministers, more missionaries; I want more zeal, more earnestness." Good God, open her eyes, I pray You. Were her eyes opened she would see that in the possession of the Holy Spirit there is a well of water close to her hand, and all she craves is there—more, indeed, than she craves—a great deal more than she yet knows that she needs. Oh, for faith in the eternal Spirit, and the griefs we feel for the church of God would come to an end. II. But I must pass on. I think I hear someone say, "I have no doubt, sir, that God has provided a supply for necessities, but may I partake of that supply? may I participate in the provisions of divine love?" I will answer you by saying, in the second place, that

This Supply Is for You

Need I remind you that there are passages of Scripture which lay the provisions of the gospel singularly open? There are invitations in the Word which are not confined to any spiritual character. "The spirit and the bride say, Come. And let him who hears say, Come. And whosoever will, let him take the water of life freely." If there be any limitation there, it is *"whosoever will."* Well, but you "will." O poor soul, you would give your eyes to have Christ; you know you would. You, poor troubled, seeking one, if you had a thousand worlds you would freely forfeit them, if you could but say, "I am pardoned: my sin is blotted out." What, then, hinders you? What keeps you back? *"Whosoever will,* let him come"; and *you* will: therefore come. We are told to "preach the gospel to every creature. He who believes and is baptized shall be saved." Are you a "creature"? If so, if you believe and are baptized you shall be saved. That is God's own word to you. Prove that you are not a creature. Then I cannot speak to you. But if you are a creature, to you as a creature is that gospel sent. "Ah," I hear some say, "I was reading the other day—

> All the fitness He requireth
> Is to feel your need of Him;

and I don't feel my need as I ought; so I have not got the fitness." My dear friend, do you ever like to be interrupted in the middle of a sentence? "Oh," say you, "no; that makes me say what I did not mean. Let me finish my sentence." Well, then, let that good poet, Hart, finish his verse without interrupting him. He says—

> Let not conscience make you linger,
> Nor of fitness fondly dream;
> All the fitness he requireth
> Is to feel your need of Him.
> This He gives you;
> 'Tis the Spirit's rising beam.

You never have any sense of our need of Christ unless He gives you that sense of need. That is as much His work as full assurance is. The first breath, the first pang that indicates life, is as much the divine work as the songs of angels or perfect saints before the throne.

There is another passage that has often yielded comfort to the downcast. "Come unto me all you that labor and are heavy laden, and I will give you rest." You are "laboring," are you not? Why, you have been laboring self-righteously to make a righteousness of your own. Give up that laboring and come to Christ "heavy laden." You are loaded, are you not? Loaded with troubles, loaded with sins, loaded with weaknesses, loaded with doubts. Jesus says, "Come unto me all you who labor and are heavy laden, and I will give you rest." Does that not describe you? The water is for you, then. You "labor"; you are "heavy laden"; you are "willing"; you are a "creature." "The Son of Man is come to seek and to save that which was lost." Not long ago I tried to show you that there could not be a case of sin and misery that could not slip in there. "Lost, lost." Is that what you say of yourself? The Son of Man is come to seek and to save such.

If we were to open tomorrow a free dining house, I believe it would be necessary to put up at the door before long some kind of prohibition to prevent everybody's coming. We should have to draw a line somewhere. But I am quite certain that there is no poor man in London who was hungry who would refuse to go in if he saw no prohibition there. He would say, "If there be no special invitation for me, yet I mean to go in and try it on till there is a special prohibition against me."

I am sure that is the way with most of us. If there were a distribution to be made of gold and silver, I think most of us would go and begin to take some until there was a special order that we were not to have any. I wish that any sinner who is troubled about election, for instance, would wait till God tells him he is not elected, or, if he has any misgiving about whether he may come to Christ, he would wait till he finds a passage which tells him that he may not come.

Will you also find somewhere in this world a sinner who did try to come to Christ, yet Christ would not have him. If you have ever found one of the sort, bring him here; for we have been boasting here very loudly that none ever did come to Christ whom He cast away. If you will find one who did come, and to whom Christ said, "No, no; you are not one of those I died for, not one of those I chose"; if you will find us one of the sort, we shall be sorrowfully glad to see him—glad because we would be glad to know the truth, but very sorrowful to think that that should be the truth.

No, we defy Satan to find one in hell who cried to Christ for mercy, and cast himself upon the Savior, and yet was rejected! All the demons of the pit, if they search to all eternity, cannot find such an instance. There never was, there never shall be one. Stand not back, then, you who are athirst. When you see the water, the living water, do not stand back, but freely come and take; for whosoever takes of it God will make him freely welcome, and the angels will rejoice concerning him. The water is for *you*—assuredly for you. III. Now to our last point:

It Is Available Without Any Extraordinary Exertion

Hagar went and filled her bottle with water, and she gave her child to drink. No hydraulic inventions were required; no exceedingly difficult pumping, no mechanical contrivances to obtain the water when the spring was perceived. She did a very simple thing: she held her bottle in the water till it was full, poured out into the child's mouth, and the dilemma which had threatened life was over.

Now, the way by which we get a hold of Christ is faith. A great many questions are asked about what faith is, and there are large books written about it. If you want to study the philosophy of faith till you are bewildered, read a book about faith; but if you really would know its latent power and its potent charm, put your trust in Christ, and you have all the faith that is wanted, and that too in vital energy. There are some who hold that the intrinsic virtue lies in the personal appropriation; so they say that faith is to believe that Christ died for me. These same persons tell us, "He died for everybody; consequently He must have died for me."

I do not see anything of a saving character in that belief at all. That does not appear to me to be in any degree the faith of God's elect. Properly, faith is a belief of God—what God says and what God promises. Its practical outcome is a reliance upon the *ipse dixit* of the Almighty. "Thus saith the Lord" is the warrant of faith. What is it? It is trust; and whosoever trusts Christ is saved. I am leaning here now, all my weight, and if this rail gives way I must go down; I am leaning here. Well, now, that is like faith in Christ. Lean right on Him; lean on Him with all your weight: lean hard; have no other confidence; throw yourself on Him. It is not faith to put one foot on Christ as the angel put one foot on the land, and then to put the other foot on our works as the angel put his other foot on the sea. To rest *both feet on Christ* that is faith. It is to do as the man said he did: he fell right down flat on the promise; "and then," said he, "when I am down there I can't fall not no lower." Nor you, if you are flat on the promise. God has said it: that is truth, and I believe it; and I expect Him to fulfill it.

This is the testimony that God has given concerning His Son—that we have everlasting life in Him, and if we trust Him we are saved. "But I cannot believe," says one. "Cannot believe" what? Do you say you cannot believe God? Nay, but man, when has God ever lied? Find me once when He has forfeited His word; find me once when He has broken His promise. If you say, "I cannot believe Him," do you not see that in that incredulity you have maligned God? You have blasphemed Him: you have made him a liar.

That is exactly what the Scripture says: "He that believeth not hath made God a liar." "But it seems too good to be believed," says one, "that God for Christ's sake forgives men simply on their trusting Christ." Yes, it is good. But then we have a good God, a great God. Can you not believe it when God says it? Do you feel in your heart, "Why I must believe it if God says it." Then, beloved, if you trust on Christ because God has said it, you have the faith which is the gift of God, the faith which is the work of the Holy Spirit; for this is *the* work of God, the greatest work that He does in us, that we believe in Jesus Christ whom He has sent.

"It is so simple," says one: yes, and that is the reason why it is so hard. If it were hard, people would do it; but because it is so simple they won't have it. It was a very hard thing to Naaman to go and wash in the Jordan; and why hard? Because it was so easy. If it had been a difficult thing it would not have been hard; he would have done it. "If the prophet had bid thee do some great thing, wouldst thou not have done it?" But when he says, "Wash, and be clean," oh, that is hard: and so it is here, because we are proud; that is the hardness of it. It is hard to trust Christ, because we are self-righteous; because we want to have a finger in this ourselves. But, oh, when the Spirit of God cuts us down to the ground, takes away all power, and strength, and merit, and boasting, and glorying, then it seems a blessed thing to have nothing to do but just to put the bottle in the water, and let the blessed water of life go gurgling into it till it fills up to the brim.

I think I hear another person say, "Well, but surely there is repentance: we must repent if we would be saved." Truly so, but I would put it rather thus—he who is saved always repents: repentance and faith go together; they are born at the same time; they will accompany every Christian as long as he is in this life; but take care that you do not make a mistake about what repentance is. There is a law-work which some believers feel, but that is not repentance; it is quite another thing over and above repentance. There are dark thoughts and horrid forebodings, but those are not repentance; they may or they may not be of advantage to the Christian after he has passed through them, but they are not repentance.

Repentance is simply the consciousness of sin, and the loathing of sin; and if you have these—and they are the gift of God, always the gift of God—then do not chastise yourself because you have not all the dark feelings of all the good men who ever lived. Why should you want more midnight? You are dark enough, poor soul, without fretting for more darkness. Better far that you pray for more light. You have already, I will dare to say, the repentance you are sighing after, for I know you hate sin, and you loathe yourself to think you should be a sinner at all, and you would do anything to be rid of sin—to escape from it. Would not you be glad to suffer anything if you could be perfect? If know you would. Well, that is repentance: that is the sign of repentance within your soul.

"Well," says one, "but we must pray, you know." Yes, granted. Every saved soul prays. But look here: do you know what prayer is? Do you think that prayer consists in the attitude of the body, or the ordering of the speech, or the utterance of petitions for a quarter of an hour, as I may have done in the course of the present service? I grieve to say that I may have done all that custom required in that fashion, and not have prayed at all; but it is true prayer if you can only look up to God and sigh, or if your heart does but groan before Him. Do not think that it is necessary to use fine expressions; far from it. "God be merciful to me a sinner" was the prayer that brought justification to the publican; and some of the best prayers that have ever reached God's ears are the shortest prayers that ever escaped man's lips.

Do not measure prayers by their length, I beseech you. God will help you to pray; prayer is His gift. If you cast yourself on Christ, sink or swim, throwing everything away, even your own prayers, and your own repentance—if you do come and rest on what Christ is, and what He has done, you cannot perish. Look not within you; there is nothing but blackness there. If you look within, expect to despair; but look yonder to the cross on Calvary. There is life in a look at Him.

O my dear hearers, how I wish we all looked at Him this moment! I have no hope but what I find there in those dear wounds, and in that head bowed down with anguish. "All my hope in thee is stayed, O Christ of God, made sin for me, my Substitute and Ransom! And every eye that is now looking to that Christ, and every heart that is trusting in that Christ, has salvation. There is salvation in none other. "There is none other name given under heaven whereby you must be saved"; but there is life for a look at Him.

God grant you grace to look at Him. "The word is nigh thee," on your lip and your heart. "If with your heart you believe in the Lord Jesus, and with your mouth you make confession of Him, you shall be saved." Oh, that God would open the eyes of many a Hagar; let her see that there is the water, that the water is free to her, and that she has but to dip in her bottle and fill it to the full.

I have used an illustration here before, but I cannot think of a better one. At the risk of repetition therefore, I will give it to you again. It just illustrates the case of many persons here present. I heard that a vessel, after having crossed the Atlantic, had arrived in the mouth of the great river Amazon without being aware that it was there. The water was all spent, and they were ready to die of thirst. They sighted another vessel, and ran up the signal, and when the vessel came within hail of them she said, "What do you want?" The answer went back, "Water! We are dying for water." And you may imagine their surprise when there came across the waves this sound—"Dip it up. You are in a fresh-water river." They had nothing to do but to throw the bucket overboard, and get as much as ever they would.

So likewise there is many a sinner crying, "What must I do to be saved? Oh, what hard thing shall I bear? What sharp thing shall I feel? What expensive thing shall I give? What tedious work shall I do?" God's answer is, "Throw the bucket of faith overboard, man. It is all around you. It is nigh you. You are floating on a stream of mercy. You are in a shoreless river of grace. If you believe that Jesus is the Christ, you are born of God. If you trust yourself with Jesus, your sins, which are many, are forgiven. Go in peace, and God grant you grace to give to Him the glory through all your remaining days.

May God bless these wandering words of mine to the consolation of some of His mourners, and my heart shall give Him praise, and your hearts shall overflow with gratitude! Amen.

4

*The Allegories of Sarah and Hagar**

These are the two covenants (Galatians 4:24).

There cannot be a greater difference in the world between two things than there is between law and grace. And yet, strange to say, while the things are diametrically opposed and essentially different from each other, the human mind is so depraved, and the intellect, even when blessed by the Spirit, has become so turned aside from right judgment, that one of the most difficult things in the world is to discriminate properly between law and grace. He who knows the difference, and always recollects it—the essential difference between law and grace—has grasped the marrow of divinity. He is not far from understanding the gospel theme in all its ramifications, its outlets, and its branches, who can properly tell the difference between law and grace. There is always in a science some part which is very simple and easy when we have learned it, but which, in the commencement, stands like a high threshold before the porch.

Now, the first difficulty in striving to learn the gospel is this. Between law and grace there is a difference plain enough to every Christian, and especially to every enlightened and instructed one; but still, when most enlightened and instructed, there is always a tendency in us to confound the two things. They are as opposite as light and darkness, and can no more agree than fire and water; yet man will be perpetually striving to make a compound of them—often ignorantly, and sometimes willfully. They seek to blend the two, when God has positively put them asunder.

We shall attempt this morning to teach you something of the allegories of Sarah and Hagar, that you may thereby better understand the essential difference between the covenants of law and grace. We shall not go fully into the subject, but shall only give such illustrations of it as the text may

* This sermon is taken from *The New Park Street Pulpit* and was preached on Sunday morning, March 2, 1856.

45

furnish us. First, I shall want you to notice *the two women*, whom Paul uses as types—Hagar and Sarah; then I shall notice *the two sons*—Ishmael and Isaac; in the third place, I shall notice *Ishmael's conduct to Isaac*; and I shall conclude by noticing *the different fates of the two*. I. First, we invite you to notice

The Two Women—Hagar and Sarah

It is said that they are the types of the two covenants; and before we start we must not forget to tell you what the covenants are. The first covenant for which Hagar stands, is the covenant of works, which is this: "There is my law, O man; if you on your side will engage to keep it, I, on my side will engage that you shall live by keeping it. If you will promise to obey my commands perfectly, wholly, fully, without a single flaw, I will carry you to heaven. But mark me, if you violate one command, if you rebel against a single ordinance, I will destroy forever."

That is the Hagar covenant—the covenant propounded on Sinai, amidst tempests, fire and smoke—or rather, propounded, first of all, in the garden of Eden, where God said to Adam, "In the day that thou eatest thereof thou shalt surely die." As long as he did not eat of the tree, but remained spotless and sinless, he was most assuredly to live. That is the covenant of the law, the Hagar covenant.

The Sarah covenant is the covenant of grace, not made with God and man, but made with God and Christ Jesus, which covenant is this: "Christ Jesus on His part engages to bear the penalty of all His people's sins, to die, to pay their debts, to take their iniquities upon His shoulders; and the Father promises on His part that all for whom the Son dies shall most assuredly be saved; that seeing they have evil hearts, He will put His law in their hearts, that they shall not depart from it, and that seeing they have sins, He will pass them by and not remember them any more forever." The covenant of works was, "Do this and live, O man!" but the covenant of grace is, "Do this, O Christ, and you shall live, O man!"

The difference of the covenants rests here. The one was made with man, the other with Christ; the one was a conditional covenant, conditional on Adam's standing, the other is a conditional covenant with Christ, but as perfectly unconditional with us. There are no conditions whatever in the covenant of grace, or if there be conditions, the covenant gives them. The covenant gives faith, gives repentance, gives good works, gives salvation, as a purely gratuitous unconditional act; nor does our continuance in that covenant depend in the least degree on ourselves. The covenant was made by God with Christ, signed, sealed, and ratified, in all things ordered well.

Now come and look at the allegory. First, I would have you notice, that *Sarah who is the type of the new covenant of grace, was the original wife of Abraham*. Before he knew anything about Hagar, Sarah was his wife.

The covenant of grace was the original covenant after all. There are some bad theologians who teach that God made man upright, and made a covenant with him; that man sinned, and that as a kind of afterthought God made a new covenant with Christ for the salvation of His people. Now, that is a complete mistake. The covenant of grace was made before the covenant of works; for Christ-Jesus, before the foundation of the world, did stand as its head and representative; and we are said to be elect according to the foreknowledge of God the Father, through the obedience and sprinkling of the blood of Jesus. Long ere we fell, we were loved of God; He did not love us out of pity to us, but He loved His people, considered purely as creatures. He loved them when they became sinners; but when He started with them He considered them as creatures. He allowed them to fall into sin, to show forth the riches of His grace, which existed before their sin. He did not love them and choose them from among the rest, after their fall, but He loved them beyond their sin, and before their sin.

He made the covenant of grace before we fell by the covenant of works. If you could go back to eternity and ask which is the oldest born, you would hear that grace was born before law—that it came into the world long before the law was promulgated. Older even than the fundamental principles which guide our morals is that great fundamental rock of grace, in covenant made of old, lone before seers preached the law, and long before Sinai smoked. Long before Adam stood in the garden God had ordained His people to eternal life, that they might be saved through Jesus.

Notice next: *though Sarah was the elder wife, yet Hagar bare the first son.* So the first man Adam was the son of Hagar; though he was born perfectly pure and spotless, he was not the son of Sarah when he was in the garden. Hagar had the first son. She bore Adam, who lived for a time under the covenant of works. Adam lived in the garden on this principle. Sins of commission were to be his fall; and if he omitted to do the sin, then he was to stand forever. Adam had it entirely in his own power whether he would obey God or not: his salvation, then, rested simply on this basis, "If you touch that fruit you die; if you obey my command, and do not touch it, you shall life." And Adam, perfect as he was, was but an Ishmael, and not an Isaac, till after his fall. *Apparently*, at any rate, he was a Hagarene, though *secretly*, in the covenant of grace, he may have been child of promise. Blessed be God, we are not under Hagar now; we are not under the law since Adam fell. Now Sarah has brought forth children. The new covenant is, "The mother of us all."

But notice again, *Hagar was not intended to be a wife; she never ought to have been anything but a handmaid to Sarah.* The law was never intended to save men: it was only designed to be a handmaid to the covenant of grace. When God delivered the law on Sinai, it was apart from His ideas that any man would ever be saved by it; He never conceived that man would attain perfection thereby. But you know that the law is a wondrous handmaid to grace. Who brought us to the Savior? Was it not the law thundering in our ears? We should never have come to Christ if the law had not driven us there; we should never have known sin if the law had not revealed it.

The law is Sarah's handmaid to sweep our hearts, and make the dust fly so that we may cry for blood to be sprinkled that the dust may be laid. The law is, so to speak, Jesus Christ's dog, to go after His sheep, and bring them to the Shepherd; the law is the thunderbolt which frightens ungodly men, and makes them turn from the error of their ways, and seek after God. Ah! if we know rightly how to use the law, if we understand how to put her in her proper place, and make her obedient to her mistress, then all will be well. But this Hagar will always be wishing to be mistress, as well as Sarah; and Sarah will never allow that, but will be sure to treat her harshly, and drive her out. We must do the same; and let none murmur at us, if we treat the Hagarenes harshly in these days—if we sometimes speak hard things against those who are trusting in the works of the law.

We will quote Sarah as an example. *She* treated Hagar harshly, and so will we. We mean to make Hagar flee into the wilderness: we wish to have nothing to do with her. Yet it is very remarkable, that coarse and ill-featured as Hagar is, men have always a greater love for her than they have for Sarah; and they are prone continually to be crying, "Hagar, you shall be my mistress," instead of saying, "Nay, Sarah, I will be your son, and Hagar will be bondmaid."

What is God's law now? It is not *above* a Christian—it is *under* a Christian. Some men hold God's law like a rod *in terrorem*, over Christians, and say, "If you sin you will be punished with it." It is not so. The law is under a Christian; it is for him to walk on, to be his guide, his rule, his pattern. "We are not under the law, but under grace." Law is the road which guides us, not the rod which drives us, nor the spirit which actuates us. The law is good and excellent, if it keeps its place. Nobody finds fault with the handmaid, because she is not the wife; and no one shall despise Hagar because she is not Sarah. If she had but remembered her office, it had been all well, and her mistress had never driven her out. We do not wish to drive the law out of chapels, as long as it is kept in its right position; but when it is set up as mistress, away with her; we will have nothing to do with legality.

Again: *Hagar never was a free woman, and Sarah never was a slave.* So, beloved, the covenant of works never was free, and none of her children ever were. All those who trust in works never are free, and never can be, even could they be perfect in good works. Even if they have no sin, still they are bondslaves, for when we have done all that we ought to have done, God is not our debtor, we are debtors still to Him, and still remain as bondslaves. If I could keep all God's law, I should have no right to favor, for I should have done no more than was my duty, and be a bondslave still. The law is the most rigorous master in the world, no wise man would love its service; for after all you have done, the law never gives you a "Thank you," for it, but says, "Go on, sir, go on!"

The poor sinner trying to be saved by law is like a blind horse going around and around a mill, and never getting a step further, but only being whipped continually; yea, the faster he goes the more work he does, the more he is tired, so much the worse for him.

The better legalist a man is, the more sure he is of being damned; the more holy a man is, if he trust to his works, the more he may rest assured of his own final rejection and eternal portion with Pharisees. Hagar was a slave; Ishmael, moral and good as he was, was nothing but a slave, and never could be more. Not all the works he ever rendered to his father could make him a free-born son.

Sarah never was a slave. She might be sometimes taken prisoner by Pharaoh, but she was not a slave then; her husband might sometimes deny her, but she was his wife still; she was soon owned by her husband, and Pharaoh was soon obliged to send her back. So the covenant of grace might seem once in jeopardy, and the representative of it might cry, "My Father, if it be possible, let this cup pass from me"; but it never was in real hazard. And sometimes the people under the covenant of grace may seem to be captives and bondslaves; but still they are free. Oh! that we knew how to "stand fast in the liberty wherewith Christ has made us free."

One thought more. *Hagar was cast out, as well as her son; but Sarah never was.* So the covenant of works has ceased to be a covenant. Not only have the people been cast away who trusted in it, not simply was Ishmael cast out, but Ishmael's mother too. So the legalist may not only know himself to be damned, but the law as a covenant has ceased to be, for mother and son are both driven out by the gospel, and those who trust in law are sent away by God. You ask today who is Abraham's wife? Why Sarah; does she not sleep side by side with her husband in the Machpelah's cave at this instant? There she lies, and if she lie there for a thousand years to come, she will still be Abraham's wife, while Hagar never can be.

Oh, how sweet to think, that the covenant made of old was in all things ordered well, and never, never shall be removed. "Although my house be not so with God, yet hath he made with me an everlasting covenant, ordered in all things and sure." Ah! you legalists, I do not wonder that you teach the doctrine of falling away, because that is consistent with your theology. Of course, Hagar has to be driven out, and Ishmael too. But we who preach the covenant of free and full salvation know that Isaac never shall be driven out, and that Sarah never shall cease to be the friend and wife of Abraham. You Hagarenes! Ceremonialists! Hypocrites! Formalists! of what avail will it be, when at last you shall say, "Where is my mother?

Where is my mother, the law?" Oh! she is driven out, and you may go with her into eternal oblivion. But where is my mother? The Christian can say at last; and it will be said, "There is the mother of the faithful, Jerusalem above, the mother of us all; and we shall enter in, and dwell with our Father and our God." II. Now we are going to review

The Two Sons

While the two women were types of the two covenants, the two sons were types of those who live under each covenant. Isaac is a type of the man who walks by faith, and not by sight, and who hopes to be saved by grace; Ishmael of the man who lives by works, and hopes to be saved by his own good deeds. Let us look at these two.

First, *Ishmael is the elder.* So beloved, the legalist is a great deal older than the Christian. If I were a legalist today, I should be some fifteen or sixteen years older than I am as a Christian, for we are all born legalists. It is grace that turns us into Calvinists, grace that makes Christians of us, grace that makes us free, and makes us know our standing in Christ Jesus. The legalist must be expected, then, to have more might of argument than Isaac; and when the two boys are wrestling, of course Isaac generally gets a fall, for Ishmael is the biggest fellow. And you must expect to hear Ishmael making the most noise, for he is to be a wild man, his hand against every man, and every man's hand against him; whereas Isaac is a peaceful lad. He always stands up for his mother, and when he is mocked, he can go and tell his mother that Ishmael mocked him, but that is all that he can do; he has not much strength.

So you notice now-a-days. The Ishmaelites are generally the strongest, and they can give us desperate falls when we get into argument with them. In fact, it is their boast and glory that the Isaacs have not much power of reasoning—not much logic. No, Isaac does not want it, for he is an heir according to promise, and promise and logic do not much consist together. His logic is his faith; his rhetoric is his earnestness. Never expect the gospel to be victorious when you are disputing after the manner of men; more usually look to be beaten. If you are discoursing with a legalist, and he conquers you, say, "Ah! I expected that; it shows I am an Isaac, for Ishmael will be sure to give Isaac a thrashing, and I am not at all sorry for it. Your father and mother were in the prime of life, and were strong; and it was natural that you should overcome me, for my father and mother were quite old people."

But where was the *difference* between the two lads in their outward appearance? There was *no difference between them as to ordinances*, for both of them were circumcised. There was no distinction with regard to outward and visible signs. So, my dearly beloved, there is often no difference between Ishmael and Isaac, between the legalist and the Christian, in matters of outward ceremonies. The legalist takes the sacrament and is baptized;

he would be afraid to die if he did not. And *I do not believe there was much difference as to character.* Ishmael was nearly as good and honorable as Isaac; there is nothing said against him in Scripture; indeed, I am led to believe that he was an especially good lad, from the fact that when God gave a blessing, he said, "With Isaac shall the blessing be." Abraham said, "O that Ishmael might live before you." He cried to God for Ishmael, because he loved the lad, doubtless, for his disposition. God said, yes, I will give Ishmael such-and-such a blessing; he shall be the father of princes, he shall have temporal blessings; but God would not turn aside, even for Abraham's prayer. And when Sarah was rather fierce, as she must have been that day when she turned Hagar out of the house, it is said, "It grieved Abraham because of his son." And I do not suspect that Abraham's attachment was a foolish one. There is one trait in Ishmael's character that you love very much. When Abraham died, he did not leave Ishmael a single stick or stone, for he had previously given him his portion and sent him away; yet he came to his father's funeral, for it is said that his sons Ishmael and Isaac buried him in Machpelah. There seems then to have been but little difference in the characters of the two. So, dearly beloved, there is little difference between the legalist and the Christian as to the outward walk. They are both the visible sons of Abraham. It is not a distinction of life; for God allowed Ishmael to be as good as Isaac, in order to show that it was not the goodness of man that made any distinction, but that He "will have mercy on whom he will have mercy, and whom he will he hardeneth."

Then *what was the distinction*? Paul has told us that the first was born after the *flesh*, and the second after the *Spirit*. The first was a natural son, the other a spiritual one. Ask the legalist, "You do good works; you have repented, you say: you are keeping the law, and you have no need to repent. Now, where did you get your strength from?" Perhaps he says, "Grace." But if you ask him what he means, he says that he used it; he had grace, but he used it. Then the difference is, *you* used your grace, and others did not. Yes. Well, then, it is your own doing. You may call it grace, or you may call it mustard; it was no grace after all, for it was your using, you say, that made the difference. But ask poor Isaac how he has kept the law, and what does he say? Very badly, indeed. Are you a sinner, Isaac? "Oh! yes, an exceedingly great one; I have rebelled against my father times without number; I have often gone astray from him." Then you do not think yourself quite as good as Ishmael, do you? "No." But yet there is a difference between you and him after all. What has made the difference? "Why, grace has made me to differ." Why is not Ishmael an Isaac? Could Ishmael have been an Isaac? "No," says Isaac, "it was God who made me to differ, from the first to the last; He made me a child of promise before I was born, and He must keep me so."

Grace all the work shall crown
Through everlasting days;
It lays in heaven the topmost stone,
And well deserves the praise.

Isaac has more really good works; he does not stand second to Ishmael. When he is converted, he labors, if it be possible, to serve his father far more than the legalist does his master; but still doubltess, if you were to hear both their tales, you would hear Isaac say that he was a poor miserable sinner, while Ishmael would make himself out a very honorable Pharisaic gentleman. The difference is not in *works*, however, but in *motives*; not in the life, but in the means of sustaining life—not in what they do, so much as in how they do it. Here, then, is the difference between some of you. Not that you legalists are worse than Christians; you may be often better in your lives, and yet you may be lost. Do you complain of that as unjust? Not in the least. God says men must be saved by faith, and if you say, "No, I will be saved by works," you may try it, but you will be lost forever. It is as if you had a servant, and you should say, "John, go and do such-and-such a thing in the stable"; but he goes away and does the reverse, and then says, "Sir, I have done it very nicely." "Yes," you say, "but that is not what I told you to do." So God has not told you to work out your salvation by good works; but He has said, "Work out your own salvation with fear and trembling, for it is God that works in you to will and to do of his good pleasure." So that when you come before God with your good works He will say, "I never told you to do that. I said, believe on the Lord Jesus Christ, and be baptized, and you shall be saved," "Ah!" you say, "I thought the other was a great deal better way." Sir, you will be lost for your thoughts. "Why is it that the Gentiles, who followed not after righteousness, have attained unto righteousness," when Israel, who followed after righteousness, has not attained it? It is this: "Because they sought it not by faith, but by the works of the law." III. Now I will briefly say a word of two concerning

Ishmael's Conduct to Isaac

Have not some of you, dear sons of Hagar, felt exceedingly irritated when you heard this doctrine? You have said, "It is dreadful, it is horrible, it is quite unjust, that I may be as good as I like, but if I am not a son of the promise, I cannot be saved; it is really awful, it is an immoral doctrine; it does a deal of damage, and ought to be stopped." Of course! That shows that you are an Ishmael. Of course Ishmael will mock at Isaac; and we need no further explanation. Where the pure sovereignty of God is preached, where it is held that the child of the promise, and not the child of the flesh, is the heir, the child of the flesh always makes a hubbub about it. What said Ishmael to Isaac? "What business have you here? Am I not my father's eldest son? I should have had all the property, if it had not been for you. Are you above me?" that is how the legalist talks. "Is not God the father of everybody? Are we not all His children? He ought not to make any difference." Said Ishmael: "Am not I as good as you? Do I not serve my father as well? As for you, you know you are your mother's favorite, but my mother is as good as yours." And so he teased and mocked at Isaac. That is just how some do with free salvation. The legalist says, "I don't see it, I cannot have it, and I won't; if we are both equal in character, it cannot be fair that one should be lost, and the other saved." Thus he mocks at free grace. You may get on very easily, if you do not preach free grace too fully, but if you dare to speak such things, though they are obnoxious to the crowd, what will people say? They call them "baits for popularity." Few fishes, however, bite at those baits. Most men say, "I hate him, I cannot bear him; he is so uncharitable."

You say we preach this to gain popularity! Why, it is, upon the surface of it, a bare-faced lie; for the doctrine of God's sovereignty will always be unpopular; men will always hate it, and grind their teeth, just as they did when Jesus taught it. Many widows He said, were in Israel, but to none of them was the prophet sent, save unto a widow of Sarepta. And many lepers were in Israel, but none of them were healed, except one who came from far away Syria. A fine popularity our Savior got from that sermon. The people ground their teeth at Him; and all the popularity He had, would have been to be pushed down the hill, from which, it is said, they would have cast Him headlong, but He made His way out of them and escaped. What! *popular* to humble a man's pride, to abolish man's standing, and make Him cringe before God as a poor sinner! No; it will never be popular till men be born angels, and all men love the Lord, and that will not be just yet, I ween. IV. But we have to inquire

What Became of the Two Sons?

First, *Isaac had all the inheritance, and Ishmael none.* Not that Ishmael came off poorly, for he had many presents, and became very rich and great in this world; but he had no spiritual inheritance. So the legalist will get many blessings, as a reward for his legality; he will be respected and honored. "Verily," said Christ, "the Pharisees have their reward." God does not rob any man of his reward. Whatever a man angles for, he catches. God pays men all He owes, and a great deal over; and those who keep His law, even in this world, will receive great favors. By obeying God's command they will not injure their bodies as much as the vicious, and they will preserve their reputation better—obedience does good in this way. But then Ishmael had none of the inheritance. So, poor legalist, if you are depending on your works, or on anything, except the free sovereign grace of God, for your deliverance from death, you will not have so much as a foot of the inheritance of Canaan, but in that great day when God shall allot the portions of all the sons of Jacob, there will be not a scrap for you. But if you are a poor Isaac, a poor guilty trembling sinner—and if you say, "Ishmael has his hands full,

But nothing in my hands I bring,
Simply to the cross I cling,

If you are saying this morning—

I am nothing at all,
But Jesus Christ is my all in all.

If you renounce all the works of the flesh, and confess, "I the chief of sinners am, but I am the child of the promise; and Jesus died for me," you shall have an inheritance, and you shall not be robbed of it by all the mocking Ishmaels in the world; nor shall it be diminished by the sons of Hagar. You may sometimes be sold, and carried down to Egypt, but God will bring His Josephs and His Isaacs back again, and you shall yet be exalted to glory, and sit on Christ's right hand.

Ah! I have often thought what consternation there will be in hell when outwardly good men go there. "Lord," says one as he goes in, "am I to go into that loathsome dungeon? Did not I keep the Sabbath? Was I not a strict Sabbatarian? I never cursed or swore in all my life. Am I to go there? I paid tithes of all that I possessed, and am I to be locked up there? I was baptized; I took the Lord's supper; I was everything that ever a man could be, that was good. It is true, I did not believe in Christ; but I did not think I needed Christ, for I thought I was too good and too honorable; and am I to be locked up there?" Yes, sir! and among the damned you shall have this preeminence, that you scorned Christ most of all. They never set up an anti-Christ. They followed sin, and so did you in measure, but you did add to your sin this most damnable of sins: that you set up yourself as an anti-Christ, and bowed down and worshiped your own fancied goodness.

Then God will proceed to tell the legalist, "On such a day I heard you rail at My sovereignty; I heard you say it was unfair of Me to save My people, and distribute My favors after the counsel of My own will; you did impugn your Creator's justice, and justice you shall have in all its power." The man had thought he had a great balance on his side, but he finds it is only some little grain of duty; but then God holds up the immense roll of his sins, with this at the bottom: "Without God, without hope, a stranger from the commonwealth of Israel!" The poor man then sees that his little treasure is not half a mite, while God's great bill is ten thousand million talents; and so with an awful howl, and a desperate shriek, he runs away with all his little notes of merit that he had hoped would have saved him. He is crying, "I am lost! I am lost with all my good works! I find my good works were sands, but my sins were mountains; and because I had not faith, all my righteousness was but white-washed hypocrisy."

Now, once more, *Ishmael was sent away, and Isaac was kept in the house.* So there are some of you, when the searching day shall come to try

God's church, though you have been living in the church as well as others, though you have the mask of profession on you, you will find that it will not avail. You have been like the elder son; whenever a poor prodigal has come into the church, you have said, "As soon as your son is come who has devoured his living with harlots, you have killed for him the fatted calf." Ah! envious legalist, you will be banished at last from the house.

I tell you legalist, and formalist, that you have no more to do with Christ than the heathen have, and though you have been baptized with Christian baptism, though you sit at a Christian table, though you hear a Christian sermon, you have neither part nor lot in the matter, unless you are trusting simply in the grace of God, and are an heir according to the promise. Whosoever trusts to his works, though it be ever so little, will find that that little trust will ruin his soul. All that nature spins must be unraveled. That ship which works have built must have her keel cut in halves. A soul must trust simply and wholly to the covenant of God, or else that soul is lost.

Legalist, you hoped to be saved by works. Come, now, I will treat you respectfully. I will not charge you with having been a drunkard, or a swearer; but I want to ask you, Are you aware, that in order to be saved by works, it is requisite that you should be entirely perfect? God demands the keeping of the whole law. If you have a vessel with the smallest crack in it, it is not a whole one. Have you never committed sin in all your life? Have you never thought an evil thought, never had an evil imagination? Come, sir, I would not suppose that you have stained those white kid gloves with anything like lust, or carnality, or that your fine mouth which uses such chaste language ever condescended to an oath, or anything like lasciviousness; I will not imagine that you have ever sung a lascivious song. I will leave that out of the question—but have you never sinned? "Yes," you say. Then, mark this: *"the soul that sins, it shall die"*; and that is all I have to say. But if you will deny that you have ever sinned, do you know that if in future you commit but one sin—though you should live for seventy years a perfect life, and at the end of that seventy years should commit one sin, all your obedience would go for nothing; for *"He that offends in one point is guilty of all."* "Sir," you say, "you are going on a wrong supposition, for though I believe I ought to do some good works, I believe Jesus Christ is very merciful, and though I am not exactly perfect, I am sincere, and I think sincere obedience will be accepted instead of perfect obedience."

You do, indeed! and pray what is sincere obedience? I have known a man to get drunk once a week; he was very sincere, and he did not think he was doing wrong so long as he was sober on a Sunday. Many people have what they call a sincere obedience, but it is one which always leaves a little margin for iniquity.

But then you say, "I do not take too much margin, it is only a little sin

I allow." My dear sir, you are quite in error as to your sincere obedience, for if this be what God requires, then hundreds of the vilest characters are as sincere as you are. But I do not believe you are sincere. If you were sincere, you would obey what God says, "Believe on the Lord Jesus Christ, and thou shalt be saved." It strikes me your sincere obedience is a sincere delusion, and such you will find it. "Oh," you say, "I believe that after all we have done, we must go to Jesus Christ, and we must say, "Lord, there is a great deficiency here, will You make it up?"

I have heard of weighing witches against the parish Bible, and if they were found heavier they were declared to be innocent; but to put the witch and the Bible in the same scale is a new idea. Why, Christ will not get in the scale with such a conceited fool as you are. You wish Christ to be a make-weight. He is much obliged to you for the compliment, but He will accept no such menial service. "Oh," you say, "He shall *assist* me in the matter of salvation." Yes, I know that would please you; but Christ is a very different kind of Savior; He has a propensity when He does a thing to do it all. You may think it strange, but He never likes any assistance. When He made the world, He did not ask the angel Gabriel so much as to cool the molten matter with his wing, but He did it entirely Himself. So it is in salvation: He says, "My glory I will not give to another."

And I beg to remind you, as you profess to go to Christ, and yet to have a little share in the business yourself, that there is a passage in the Scriptures which is *apropos* to you, and which you may masticate at your leisure, "And if by grace, then is it no more of works; otherwise grace is no more grace. But if it be of works, then is it no more grace; otherwise work is no more work." For if you mix the two together, you spoil them both. Go home, sir, and make yourself a stirabout with fire and water, endeavor to keep in your house a lion and a lamb, and when you have succeeded in doing these, tell me that you have made works and grace agree, and I will tell you, you have told me a lie even then, for the two things are so essentially opposite, that it cannot be done. Whosoever among you will cast all his good works away, and will come to Jesus, with this "Nothing, *nothing*, NOTHING,

> "*Nothing* in my hands I bring,
> Simply to the cross I cling,"

Christ will give you good works enough, His Spirit will work in you to will and to do of His good pleasure, and will make you holy and perfect; but if you have endeavored to get holiness before Christ, you have begun at the wrong end, you have sought the flower before you have the root, and are foolish for your pains. Ishmaels, tremble before Him now! If others of you be Isaacs, may you ever remember that you are children of the promise. Stand fast. Do not be entangled by the yoke of bondage, for you are not under the law, but under grace.

5

Hannah: A Woman of a Sorrowful Spirit[*]

Hannah answered and said, No, my lord, I am a woman of a sorrowful spirit (1 Samuel 1:15).

The special cause of Hannah's sorrow arose from the institution of polygamy, which, although it was tolerated under the old law, is always exhibited to us in practical action as a most fruitful source of sorrow and sin. In no one recorded instance in Holy Scripture is it set forth as admirable; and in most cases the proofs of its evil effects lie open to the sun. Lamech leads the way, and he is a homicide descended of the murderous house of Cain, and the father of Tubal-cain, or Vulcan, the fashioner of weapons of destruction: never was this institution the harbinger of peace, but the favorer of strife. We ought to be grateful that under the Christian religion that abomination has been wiped away; for even with such husbands as Abraham, Jacob, David, and Solomon it did not work toward happiness or righteousness.

The husband found the system a heavy burden, grievous to be borne, for he soon found out the truth of the wise man's advice to the Sultan, "First learn to live with two tigresses, and then expect to live happily with two wives." The wife must in nearly every case have felt the wretchedness of sharing a love which ought to be all her own.

What miseries eastern women have suffered in the harem none can tell, or perhaps imagine. In the case before us, Elkanah had trouble enough through wearing the double chain, but still the heaviest burden fell upon his beloved Hannah, the better of his two wives. The worse the woman the better she could get on with the system of many wives, but the good woman, the true woman, was sure to suffer under it. Though dearly loved

---

* This sermon is taken from *The Metropolitan Tabernacle Pulpit* and was preached at the Metropolitan Tabernacle, Newington, in 1880.

by her husband, the jealousy of the rival wife embittered Hannah's life, and made her "a woman of a sorrowful spirit."

We thank God that no longer is the altar of God covered with tears, with weeping, and with crying out, of those wives of youth who find their husbands' hearts estranged and divided by other wives. Because of the hardness of their hearts the evil was tolerated for a while, but the many evils which sprang of it should suffice to put a ban upon it among all who seek the welfare of our race. In the beginning the Lord made for man but one wife. And wherefore one? For He had the residue of the spirit, and could have breathed into as many as He pleased. Malachi answers, "That he might seek a godly seed." As if it was quite clear that the children of polygamy would be ungodly, and only in the house of one man and one wife would godliness be found. This witness is of the Lord, and is true.

But enough sources of grief remain—more than enough; and there is not in any household, I suppose, however joyous, the utter absence of the cross. The worldling says, "There is a skeleton in every house." I know little about such dead things, but I know that a cross of some sort or other must be borne by every child of God. All the true-born heirs of heaven must pass under the rod of the covenant. What son is there whom the Father does not chasten? The smoking furnace is part of the insignia of the heavenly family, without which a man may well question whether he stands in covenant relationship to God at all. Probably some Hannah is now before me, smarting under the chastening hand of God, some child of light walking in darkness, some daughter of Abraham bowed down by Satan, and it may not be amiss to remind her that she is not the first of her kind, but that in years gone by there stood at the door of God's house one like her, who said of herself "No, my lord, I am a woman of a sorrowful spirit." May the ever-blessed Comforter, whose work lies mainly with the sorrowful, fill our meditation with consolation at this time. I. In speaking of this "woman of a sorrowful spirit" we shall make this first remark: that—

Much That Is Precious May Be Connected with a Sorrowful Spirit

In itself, a sorrowful spirit is not to be desired. Give us the bright eye, the cheerful smile, the vivacious manner, the genial tone. If we do not desire mirth and merriment, yet give us at least that calm peace, that quiet composure, that restful happiness which makes home happy wherever it pervades the atmosphere. There are wives, mothers, and daughters who should exhibit more of these cheerful graces than they now do, and they are very blamable for being petulant, unkind, and irritable; but there are others, I doubt not, who labor to their utmost to be all that is delightful, and yet fail in the attempt, because, like Hannah, they are of a sorrowful spirit, and cannot shake off the grief which burdens their heart.

Now, it is idle to tell the night that it should be brilliant as the day, or bid the winter put on the flowers of summer; and equally vain is it to chide the broken heart. The bird of night cannot sing at heaven's gate, nor can the crushed worm leap like a hart up on the mountains. It is of little use exhorting the willow whose branches weep by the river to lift up its head like the palm, or spread its branches like the cedar: everything must act according to its kind; each nature has its own appropriate ways, nor can it escape the bonds of its fashioning. There are circumstances of constitution, education, and surroundings which render it difficult for some very excellent persons to be cheerful: they are predestined to be known by such a name as this— "A woman of a sorrowful spirit."

Note well the precious things which went in Hannah's case with a sorrowful spirit. The first was true godliness: *she was a godly woman.* As we read the chapter, we are thoroughly certified that her heart was right with God. We cannot raise any question about the sincerity of her prayer, or her prevalence of it. We do not doubt for a moment the truthfulness of her holy joy, the confidence of her faith, or the strength of her consecration. She was one who feared God above many, an eminently gracious woman, and yet "a woman of a sorrowful spirit." Never draw the inference from sorrow that the subject of it is not beloved of God. You might more safely reason in the opposite way, though it would not be always safe to do so, for outward circumstances are poor tests of a man's spiritual state.

Certainly Dives, in his scarlet and fine linen, was not beloved of God, while Lazarus, with the dogs licking his sores, was a favorite of heaven: and yet it is not every rich man who is cast away, or every beggar who will be born aloft by angels. Outward condition can lead us to no determination one way or another. Hearts must be judged, conduct and actions must be weighed, and a verdict given otherwise than by the outward appearance.

Many persons feel very happy, but they must not therefore infer that God loves them; while certain others are sadly depressed, but it would be most cruel to suggest to them that God is angry with them. It is never said, "whom the Lord loves He enriches," but it is said, "whom the Lord loveth he chasteneth." Affliction and suffering are not proofs of sonship, for "many sorrows shall be to the wicked"; and yet, where there are great tribulations, it often happens that there are great manifestations of the divine favor. There is a sorrow of the world that results in death—a sorrow which springs from the self-will, and is nurtured in rebellion, and is therefore an evil thing, because it is opposed to the divine will. There is a sorrow which eats as does a canker, and breeds yet greater sorrows, so that such mourners descend with their sorrowful spirits down to the place where sorrow reigns supreme, and hope shall never come. Think of this, but never doubt the fact that a sorrowful spirit is in perfect consistency with the love of God, and the possession of true godliness. It is freely admitted that godliness ought to cheer many a sorrowful spirit more than it does. It is also admitted that much of the experience of Christians is not Christian experience, but a mournful departure from what true believers ought to be and feel.

There is very much that Christians experience which they never ought to experience. Half the troubles of life are homemade, and utterly unnecessary. We afflict ourselves, perhaps, ten times more than God afflicts us. We add many thongs to God's whip: when there would be but one we make nine. God sends one cloud by His providence, and we raise a score by our unbelief. But removing all that, and making the still further abatement that the gospel commands us to rejoice in the Lord always (and that it would never bid us do so if there were not abundant causes and arguments for it), yet, for all that, a sorrowful spirit may be possessed by one who most truly and deeply fears the Lord.

Never judge those whom you see sad, and write them down as under the divine anger, for you might err most grievously and most cruelly in making so rash a judgment. Fools despise the afflicted, but wise men prize them. Many of the sweetest flowers in the garden of grace grow in the shade, and flourish in the drip. True, there are children of the tropical sun, whose beauty and fragrance could only be produced by having bathed themselves in the golden flood, and these, in certain respects, must always stand in the forefront, yet are there choice flowerets to whom the unshaded sun would be death. They prefer a sheltered bank, or a ravine in the forest, under the shadow of the thick boughs, where a softened, mellowed light develops them to perfection.

I am persuaded that he "who feedeth among the lilies" has rare plants in his flora, fair and fragrant, choice and comely, which are more at home in the damps of mourning than in the glaring sun of joy. I have known such, who have been a living lesson to us all, from their brokenhearted penitence, their solemn earnestness, their jealous watchfulness, their sweet humility, and their gentle love. These are lilies of the valley, bearing a wealth of beauty pleasant even to the King Himself. Feeble as to assurance, and to be pitied for their timidity, yet have they been lovely in their despondencies, and graceful in their holy anxieties. These are not pearls with the mild radiance of peace, nor rubies with the ruddy hue of ardor, nor sapphires with the bright blue of joy, nor emeralds with the restfulness of confidence; but diamonds of the first water, incarnate drops of sorrow, clear and transparent, and soon to be set among the brightest gems in the Redeemer's diadem. Hannah, then, possessed godliness despite her sorrow.

In connection with this sorrowful spirit of hers Hannah was *a lovable woman*. Her husband greatly delighted in her. That she had no children was to him no depreciation of her value. He said, "Am not I better to you than ten sons?" He evidently felt that he would do anything in his power to uplift the gloom from her spirit. This fact is worth noting, for it does so happen that many sorrowful people are far from being lovable people. In too many instances their griefs have soured them. Their affliction has generated acid in their hearts, and with that acrid acid they bite into everything they touch; their temper has more of the oil of vitriol in it than of the oil of brotherly love. Nobody ever had any trouble except themselves, they brook no rival in the realm of suffering, but persecute their fellow sufferers with a kind of jealousy, as if they alone were the brides of suffering, and others were mere intruders. Every other person's sorrow is a mere fancy, or make-believe, compared with theirs. They sit alone, and keep silence; or when they speak, their silence would have been preferable.

It is a pity it should be so, and yet so it is that men and women of a sorrowful spirit are frequently to be met with who are unloving and unlovable. The more heartily, therefore, do I admire in true Christian people the grace which sweetens them so that the more they suffer themselves the more gentle and patient they become with other sufferers, and the more ready to bear whatever trouble may be involved in the necessities of compassion. Beloved, if you are much tried and troubled, and if you are much depressed in spirit, entreat the Lord to prevent your becoming a kill-joy to others. Remember your Master's rule, "And thou, when thou fastest, anoint thy head, and wash thy face, and that thou appear not unto men to fast."

I do not say that our Lord spoke the word with the exact meaning I am now giving to it, but it is a kindred sense. Be cheerful even when your heart is sad. There is no need that the world should be hung in black because I wear crape on my hat. It is not necessary that every heart should be heavy because I am burdened; of what use would that be to me or to anyone else? For my own part for the sake of sick and sorrowful people, I am sorry when I hear the knell from the church tower intruding a death-note into every mourner's ear, and all perhaps because some heir of glory has risen to the throne of God and of the Lamb. That bell with solemn toll, no doubt, has a voice to the careless, and so far so good, but as the stern voice of melancholy, it is an offense against Christianity, importing that all death is doleful, and causing the sick upon their beds to feel more mournful than needs be.

Publish good news. Ring the joy-bells as loudly as you will; but there is no particular need to be everlastingly pestering everyone with your griefs. No, let us try to be cheerful that we may be lovable, even if we still remain of a sorrowful spirit. Self and our own personal woes must not be our life-psalm, nor our daily discourse. Others must be thought of, and in their joys we must try to sympathize. Patience must put self into the background, and love must bring our friends to the front. We have a God to serve, an age to bless, a family to train, a circle of friends to benefit; and these things must none of them be disregarded. If we thus put duty before complaining, and the doing of good before the craving for sympathy, we shall win much love, and among those who are prized and sought after none will be preferred to the man or woman of a sorrowful spirit.

In Hannah's case, too, the woman of a sorrowful spirit was *a very gentle woman*. Peninnah with her harsh, and haughty, and arrogant speech vexed her sore to make her fret, but we do not find that she answered her. At the annual festival, when Peninnah had provoked her most, she stole away to the sanctuary to weep alone, for she was very tender and submissive. When Eli said, "How long will you be drunken? put away your wine," she did not answer him tartly, as she might well have done. Her answer to the aged priest is a model of gentleness. She most effectually cleared herself, and plainly refuted the harsh imputation, but she made no retort, and murmured no charge of injustice. She did not tell him that he was ungenerous in having thought so harshly, nor was there anger in her grief. She excused his mistake. He was an old man. It was his duty to see that worship was fitly conducted, and, if he judged her to be in a wrong state, it was but faithfulness on his part to make the remark; and she took it, therefore, in the spirit in which she thought he offered it. At any rate, she bore the rebuke without resentment or repining.

Now, some sad people are very tart, very sharp, very severe, and, if you misjudge them at all, they condemn your cruelty with the utmost bitterness. You are the unkindest of men if you think them less than perfect. With what an air and tone of injured innocence will they vindicate themselves! You have committed worse than blasphemy if you have ventured to hint a fault. I am not about to blame them, for we might be as ungentle as they if we were to be too severe in our criticism on the sharpness which springs of sorrow; but it is very beautiful when the afflicted are full of sweetness and light, and like the sycamore figs are ripened by their bruising. When their own bleeding wound makes them tender of wounding others, and their own hurt makes them more ready to bear what of hurt may come through the mistakes of others, then have we a lovely proof that "sweet are the uses of adversity."

Dear friends, whether you are men or women of a sorrowful spirit, will you kindly recollect that your infirmity is likely to be peevishness, and that your temptation will probably be toward sharpness of temper? Therefore, watch against these things, and ask God especially to give you a gentle spirit and a quiet tongue. Look at your Lord. Oh that we all would look at Him, who when He was reviled reviled not again, and who, when they mocked Him, had not a word of condemnation, but answered by His prayers, saying, "Father, forgive them, for they know not what they do." Know this: much that is precious may go with a sorrowful spirit!

There was more, however, than I have shown you, for Hannah was *a thoughtful woman*, for her sorrow drove her first within herself, and next into much communion with her God. That she was a highly thoughtful woman appears in everything she says. She does not pour out that which first comes to hand. The product of her mind is evidently that which only a cultivated soil could yield. I will not just now speak of her song, further than to say that for loftiness of majesty and true poetry it is equal to anything from the pen of that sweet psalmist of Israel, David himself. The Virgin Mary evidently followed in the wake of this great poetess, this mistress of the lyric art.

Remember, also, that though she was a woman of a sorrowful spirit, she was *a blessed woman*. I might fitly say of her, "Hail, you who are highly favored! The Lord is with you. Blessed are you among women." The daughters of Beliah could laugh and make merry, and regard her as the dust beneath their feet, but yet she had with her sorrowful spirit found grace in the sight of the Lord. There was Peninnah, with her quiver full of children, exulting over the barren mourner, yet was not Peninnah blessed, while Hannah, with all her griefs, was dear unto the Lord. She seems to be somewhat like Him of another age, of whom we read that Jabez was more honorable than his brethren because his mother bare him with sorrow.

Sorrow brings a wealth of blessing with it when the Lord consecrates it; and if one had to take his position with the merry, or with the mournful, he would do well to take counsel of Solomon, who said, "It is better to go to the house of mourning than to the house of feasting." A present flash is seen in the mirth of the world, but there is vastly more true light to be found in the griefs of Christians. When you see how the Lord sustains and sanctifies His people by their afflictions, the darkness glows into noonday.

It is now clear that much that is precious may go with a sorrowful spirit. Let none of you despise the downcast, and never think harshly of those who are sad. If we be sorrowful ourselves, let us not write bitter things against ourselves, but hope in God under all discouragements; for we shall yet praise Him who is the health of our countenance and our God. II. We come now to a second remark, which is that

Much That Is Precious May Come Out of a Sorrowful Spirit

It is not only to be found with it, but may even grow out of it. Observe, first, that through her sorrowful spirit Hannah *had learned to pray*. I will not say but what she prayed before this great sorrow struck her, but this I know, she prayed with more intensity than before when she heard her rival talk so exceeding proudly, and saw herself to be utterly despised. Oh! brothers and sisters, if you have a secret grief, learn where to carry it, and delay not to take it there. Learn from Hannah. Her appeal was to the Lord. She did not pour out the secret of her soul into mortal ear, but spread her grief before God in His own house, and in His own appointed manner. She was in bitterness of soul, and prayed to the Lord. Bitterness of soul should always be thus sweetened. Many are in bitterness of soul, but they do not pray, and therefore the taste of the wormwood remains: O that they were wise, and looked upon their sorrows as the divine call for prayer, the cloud which brings a shower of supplication! Our troubles should be rails upon which we ride to God; rough winds which hurry our barque into the haven of all-prayer. When the heart is merry we may sing psalms, but concerning the afflicted it is written, "Let him pray." Thus, bitterness of spirit may be an index of our need of prayer, and an incentive to that holy exercise.

When a live coal from off the altar touches our lips we should *preach*, but when a drop of gall falls on the lips we should *pray*. I fear, my brethren, that our best prayers are born in the house of mourning. In too many cases ease and health bring a chill over supplication, and there is a necessity for a stirring of the fire with the rough iron of trial. Many a flower reserves its odor till the rough wind waves it to and fro, and shakes out its fragrance. As a rule the tried man is the praying man; and the angel must wrestle with us in the night before we learn to hold him, and cry, "I will not let you go."

O daughter of sorrow, if in your darkened chamber you shall learn the art of prevailing with the Well-beloved, yon bright-eyed maidens, down whose cheeks no tears have ever rushed, may well envy you, for to be proficient in the art and mystery of prayer is to be as a princess with God. May God grant that if we are of a sorrowful spirit, we may in the same proportion be of a prayerful spirit; and we need scarcely desire a change.

In the next place, Hannah *had learned self-denial*. This is clear, since the very prayer by which she hoped to escape out of her great grief was a self-denying one. She desired a son, that her reproach might be removed; but if her eyes might be blessed with such a sight she would cheerfully resign her darling to be the Lord's as long as he lived. Mothers wish to keep their children about them. It is natural that they should wish to see them often. But Hannah, when most eager for a man-child, asking but for one, and that one as the special gift of God, yet does not seek him for herself, but for her God. She has it on her heart that, as soon as she has weaned him, she will take him up to the house of God and leave him there, as a dedicated child whom she can only see at certain festivals.

Read her own words: "O Lord of hosts, if thou wilt indeed look on the affliction of thine handmaid, and remember me, and not forget thine handmaid, but wilt give unto thine handmaid a man child, then I will give him unto the Lord all the days of his life, and there shall no razor come upon his head." Her heart longed not to see her boy at home, his father's daily pride, and her own hourly solace, but to see him serving as a Levite in the house of the Lord. She thus proved that she had learned self-denial. Beloved, this is one of the hardest lessons: to learn to give up what we most prize at the command of God, and to do so cheerfully. This is real self-denial, when we ourselves make the proposition, and offer the sacrifice freely, as she did. To desire a blessing that we may have the opportunity of parting with it, this is self-conquest: have we reached it? O you of a sorrowful spirit, if you have learned to crucify the flesh, if you have learned to keep under the body, if you have learned to cast all your desires and will at His feet, you have gained what a thousand times repays you for all the losses and crosses you have suffered.

Personally, I bless God for joy, I think I could sometimes do with a little more of it; but I fear, when I take stock of my whole life, that I have seldom made any real growth in grace except as the result of being digged about and deluged by the stern husbandry of pain. My leaf is greenest in showery weather: my fruit is sweetest when it has been frosted by a winter's night. Woe is me that I should have to make so humbling a confession of my own foolishness, but truth compels me thus to stand among those who ought to be ashamed. I hope that many of you are much more gracious than I am, and have made much better use of your mercies, and yet I fear that many of us must confess that they have made more headway in spiritual sailing amid the raging of the sea than in happier times. A stiff breeze brings certain of us far more help than danger, and even a tempest is not without its benediction. If we have self-denial wrought in us, however costly the process, the result abundantly repays us.

Another precious thing had come to this woman, and that was, *she had learned faith.* She had become proficient in believing promises. It is beautiful to note how at one moment she was in bitterness, but as soon as Eli had said, "Go in peace: and the God of Israel grant thee thy petition that thou has asked of him," "the woman went her way and did eat, and her countenance was no more sad." She had not yet obtained the blessing, but she was persuaded of the promise, and embraced it, after that Christly fashion which our Lord taught us when He said, "Believe that ye have the petitions which ye have asked, and ye shall have them." She wiped her tears, and smoothed the wrinkles from her brow, knowing that she was heard. By faith she held a man child in her arms, and presented him to the Lord. This is no small virtue to attain.

When a sorrowful spirit has learned to believe God, to roll its burden upon Him, and bravely to expect help from Him, it has learned by its losses how to make its best gains—by its griefs how to unfold its richest joys. Hannah is one of the honored band who through faith "received promises," therefore, O you who are of a sorrowful spirit, there is no reason why you should not also be of a believing spirit, even as she was.

Still more of preciousness this woman of a sorrowful spirit found growing out of her sorrow, but with one invaluable item I shall close the list: she had evidently *learned much of God.* Driven from common family joys she had been drawn near to God, and in that heavenly fellowship she had remained a humble waiter and watcher. In seasons of sacred nearness to the

Lord she had made many heavenly discoveries of His name and nature, as her song makes us perceive.

First, she now knew that the heart's truest joy is not in children, nor even in mercies given in answer to prayer, for she began to sing, "My heart rejoiceth in the Lord"—not "in Samuel," but in Jehovah her chief delight was found. "Mine horn is exalted in the Lord"—not "in that little one whom I have so gladly brought up to the sanctuary." No. She says in the first verse, "I rejoice in thy salvation," and it was even so. God was her exceeding joy, and His salvation her delight. O it is a great thing to be taught to put earthly things in their proper places, and when they make you glad yet to feel, "My gladness is in God; not in corn and wine and oil, but in the Lord himself; all my fresh springs are in him."

Next, she had also discovered *the Lord's glorious holiness*, for she sang, "There is none holy as the Lord." The wholeness of His perfect character charmed and impressed her, and she sang of Him as far above all others in His goodness.

She had found out *God's method in providence*, for how sweetly she sings, "The bows of the mighty men are broken, and they that stumbled are girded with strength." She knew that this was always God's way—to overturn those who are strong in self, and to set up those who are weak. It is God's way to cut down and wither the high and green trees, and to cause the low and withered trees to flourish. It is God's way to smite the strong with weakness, and to bless the weak with strength. As her great successor sang at a later day, "He hath put down the mighty from their seats, and exalted them of low degree. He hath filled the hungry with good things, and the rich he hath sent empty away" (Luke 1:52). It is God's peculiar way, and He abides by it. The full He empties, and the empty He fills. Those who boast of their power to live He slays; and those who faint before Him as dead, He makes alive. Friend, do you know anything of this? For, mark you, this is a secret which the saints know by personal experience!

She had also been taught *the way and method if His grace* as well as of His providence, for never did a woman show more acquaintance with the wonders of divine grace than she did when she sang, "He raiseth up the poor out of the dust, and lifteth up the beggar from the dunghill, to set them among princes, and to make them inherit the throne of glory." This, too, is another of those ways of the Lord which are only understood by His people. None but they will ever sing of this singular sovereignty of grace: as for the worldlings, they utterly abhor the doctrine.

She had also seen *the Lord's faithfulness* to His people. Some Christians, even in these gospel days, do not believe in the doctrine of the final perseverance of the saints but she did. She sang, "He will keep the feet of his saints"; and, beloved, so He will, or none of them will ever stand.

> If ever it could come to pass,
>> That sheep of Christ should fall away,
>> My fickle, feeble, soul, alas!
>> Would fall a thousand times a day.

But here is my comfort, and yours also, "He will keep the feet of his saints."

She had foreseen also somewhat of *His kingdom*, and of the glory of it. Her prophetic eye, made brighter and clearer by her holy tears, enabled her to look into the future, and looking her joyful heart made her sing, "He shall give strength unto his King, and exalt the horn of his Anointed."

Have I not sufficiently shown you that many precious things come out of a sorrowful spirit? III. And now, lastly,

Much That Is Precious Will Yet Be Given to Those Who Are Truly the Lord's, Even Though They Have a Sorrowful Spirit

For, first, Hannah had *her prayers answered*. Ah! little could she have imagined when Eli was rebuking her for drunkenness, that within a short time she should be there, and the same priest should look at her with deep respect and delight because the Lord had favored her. And you, my dear friend of a sorrowful spirit, would not weep so much tonight if you knew what is in store for you. You would not weep at all if you guessed how soon all will change, and like Sarah, you will laugh for very joy. You are very poor; you scarcely know where you will place your head tonight; but if you knew in how short a time you will be among the angels, your penury would not cause you much distress. You are sickening and pining away, and will soon go to your long home. You would not be so depressed if you remembered how bright around your head will shine the starry diadem, and how sweetly your tongue shall pour forth heavenly sonnets such as none can sing but those who, like you, have tasted of the bitter waters of grief. It is better on before!

It is better on before! A short way ahead the road will end or mend! Today's sailing is boisterous; but before the sun goes down, or, at least, *when* it goes down, all will be quiet, and your barque will be motionless from stem to stern. The Red Sea before you rolls uneasily, its billows threatening, but all will be as still as a stone while the Lord's people pass over; or if a sound be heard, it will only be that over the waters come the strains of harpers harping with their harps, and soon you shall forget your pains and fears, for you shall be forever with the Lord. Let these things cheer you if you are of a sorrowful spirit. There shall be a fulfillment of the things which God has promised to you. Eye has not seen, nor ear heard, the things He has laid up for you, but His Spirit reveals them to you at this hour. Be of good courage, and believe that the issues of life and death are fixed and sure; eternal love has ordained them.

Not only did there come to Hannah after her sorrow an answered prayer, but *grace to use that answer*. I do not thing that Hannah would have been a fit mother for Samuel if she had not first of all been of a sorrowful spirit. It is not everybody who can be trusted to educate a young prophet. Many a fool of a woman has made a fool of her child. He was so much her "duck" that he grew up to be a goose. It requires a wise woman to train up a wise son, and therefore I regard Samuel's eminent character and career as largely the fruit of his mother's sorrow, and as a reward for her griefs. Hannah was a thoughtful mother, which was something, and her thought induced diligence. She had slender space in which to educate her boy, for he left her early to wear the little robe, and minister before the Lord; but in that space her work was effectually done, for the child Samuel worshiped the very day she took him up to the temple.

In many of our homes we have a well-drawn picture of a child at prayer, and such I doubt not was the very image of the youthful Samuel. I like to think of him with that little coat on—that linen ephod—coming forth in solemn style, as a child-servant of God, to help in the services of the temple. I think I see a little man with his long hair all streaming down his shoulders, for by his mother's vow no razor could come upon his head; see him yourselves, and mark how he rebukes the Roman shavelings. He did not belong to that modern priesthood which, by shaving its head, implies its own fever or madness, but denies its own claim to belong to God. Let the priests shave one, and so cut themselves off from the true temple. I say it is pleasant to see how, even in the matter of his hair, his mother had trained him up in the way, so that he never departed from it: this was a great gift, and it was vouchsafed to a woman of a sorrowful spirit.

Hannah had acquired another blessing, and that was *the power to magnify the Lord*. Those sweet songs of hers, especially that precious one which we have been reading—where did she get it from? I will tell you. You have picked up a shell, have you not, by the seaside, and you have put it to your ear, and heard it sing of the wild waves? Where did it learn this music? In the deeps. It had been tossed to and fro in the rough sea until it learned to talk with a deep, soft meaning of mysterious things, which only the salt sea caves can communicate.

Hannah's poetry was born of her sorrow; and if everyone here who is of a sorrowful spirit can but learn to tune his harp as sweetly as she tuned hers, he may be glad to have passed through such griefs as she endured. We may be poets and psalmists yet in our own humble way. Trials will teach us tune and time, stanzas and verses will flow like wine from the trodden grapes, and poems grow in the furrows of our adversities. Or, if not, yet shall the Lord be praised, and His love extolled in the best terms our speech can come at; and this is worth a world of suffering.

Moreover, her sorrow *prepared her to receive further blessings,* for after the birth of Samuel she had three more sons and two daughters, God thus giving her five for the one whom she had dedicated to Him. This was grand interest for her loan: 500 percent. Parting with Samuel was the necessary preface to the reception of other little ones. God cannot bless some of us till first of all He has tried us. Many of us are not fit to receive a great blessing till we have gone through the fire. Half those who have been ruined by popularity have been so ruined because they did not undergo a preparatory course of opprobrium and shame. Half those who perish by riches do so because they had not toiled to earn them, but made a lucky hit, and became wealthy in an hour. Passing through the fire anneals the weapon which afterward is to be used in the conflict.

Hannah gained grace to be greatly favored by being greatly sorrowing. Her name stands among the highly favored women because she was deeply sorrowing. She shines a bright, particular star among the faithful, and this had not been if she had not been first a woman of a sorrowful spirit. Take up your load, my beloved. Do not become murmurers as well as mourners. Carry your cross, for it is in very truth a golden one. Carry the inward as well as the outward burden, for now for a season there is a necessity that you be in heaviness through manifold temptations, but afterward comes the comfortable fruit. Look for fair results, and meanwhile bear what the Lord appoints you without repining.

Last of all, it was by suffering in patience that she became so brave a witness for the Lord, and could so sweetly sing, "There is none holy as the Lord, neither is there any rock like our God." We cannot bear testimony unless we test the promise, and therefore happy is the one whom the Lord tests and qualifies to leave a testimony to the world that God is true. To that witness I would set my own personal seal. O that it might be mine to do so at the close of life in humble prose, as that sweet poetess Frances Ridley Havergal did in richest poesy before she entered her eternal rest. Here are some of her last lines, and with them I close:

> Master, I set my seal that thou art true;
> Of thy good promise not one thing hath failed!
> And I would send a ringing challenge forth,
> To all who know thy name, to tell it out,
> Thy faithfulness to every written word,
> Thy lovingkindness crowning all the days—
> To say and sing with me: "The Lord is good,
> His mercy is forever, and his truth
> Is written on each page of all my life"!
> Yes, there *is* tribulation, but thy power

Can blend it with rejoicing. There *are* thorns,
But they have kept us in the narrow way,
The King's highway of holiness and peace.
And there *is* chastening, but the Father's love
Flows through it; and would any trusting heart
Forego the chastening and forego the love?
And every step leads on to "more and more,"
From strength to strength thy pilgrims pass, and sing
The praise of him who leads them on and on,
From glory unto glory, even here!

6

*Remember Lot's Wife**

Remember Lot's wife (Luke 17:32).

It was the purpose of God always to maintain a testimony for truth and righteousness in the midst of this ungodly world. For this end of old He set apart for Himself a chosen family with whom He had fellowship. Abraham was the man whom God chose, that in Him and in His household the witness might be preserved. This chosen family was called out and separated from its ancestors, and led apart to dwell as wayfaring men in the land of Canaan. They were not to go into the cities and mingle with other races, but to dwell in tents as a separate tribe, lest their character should become polluted and their testimony should be silenced.

It was the Lord's intent that the people should dwell alone and not be numbered among the nations. Abraham, being called, obeyed, and went forth, not knowing whither he went. His separated life gave great exercise to his faith, and so strengthened it that it became a calm, unstaggering assurance; and this enabled him to enjoy a quiet, sublime, and happy career, dependent only upon God, and altogether above as well as apart from man.

With him was his nephew Lot, who also left Haran at the divine call, and shared with the patriarch his wanderings in Canaan and in Egypt. He was not a man of so noble a soul, but was greatly influenced by the stronger mind of his uncle Abraham. He was sincere, no doubt, and is justly called righteous Lot, but he was fitter to be a follower than a leader. He also sojourned in tents, and led the separated life, until it became necessary for him to become an independent chieftain, because the flocks and herds of the two families had so greatly multiplied that they could not well be kept together.

Then came out the weak side of Lot's character. He did not give Abraham the choice in selecting a sheep walk, but like all weak natures he

---

* This sermon is taken from *The Metropolitan Tabernacle Pulpit* and was preached on Sunday morning, August 24, 1879.

71

selfishly consulted his own advantage, and determined to go in the direction of the cities of the plain of Jordan, where well watered pastures abounded. This led to his dwelling near the cities of the plain, where crime had reached its utmost point of horrible degradation. We read that "he pitched his tent toward Sodom"; he found it convenient to be near a settled people, and to enter into friendly relations with them, though he must have known what the men of Sodom were, for the cry of them had gone forth far and wide. Thus he began to leave the separated path. After a while he went further, for one step leads to another. He was a lover of ease, and therefore he gave up the tent life, with its many inconveniences, and went to live with the townsmen of Sodom: a thing to be wondered at as well as deplored.

He did not cease to be a good man, but he did cease to be a faithful witness for his God; and Abraham seems to have given him up altogether from that day, for we find that noble patriarch inquiring of the Lord concerning his heir, saying, "Lord God, what will you give me, seeing I go childless, and the steward of my house is this Eliezer of Damascus?" And the Lord said, "This shall not be your heir." Now, this inquiry would have been needless had Lot been still reckoned to belong to the chosen seed, for naturally Lot was the heir of Abraham, but he forfeited that position and gave up his portion in the inheritance of the elect house by quitting the separated life.

Lot, although he dwelt in Sodom was not happy there, neither did he become so corrupt as to take pleasure in the wickedness of the people. Peter says that God delivered just Lot vexed with the filthy conversation of the wicked. He tried to bear his protest in the place, and signally failed, as all must do who imitate him. His witness for purity would have been far more powerful if he had kept apart from them, for this is the protest which God demands of us when he says, "Come ye out from among them, be ye separate."

In the midst of the world which lies in the wicked one Lot lived on, not without greatly degenerating in spirit, until the kings came and carried him away captive. Then by the intervention of Abraham he was delivered from the captivity which threatened him, and brought back again. This was a solemn warning, and you would have thought that Lot would have said, "I will go back to Abraham's way of living, I will again become a sojourner with God. Sodom's walls without God are far less safe than a frail tent when God is a wall of fire around it."

His vexation with the conversation of the lewd townsmen ought to have made him long for the sweet air of the wild country; but not so, he again settles down in Sodom, and forgets the holy congregation which clustered around the tent of Abraham. Being still a man of God, he could not be allowed to die in such society: it was not to be endured that "just Lot" should lay his bones in the graveyard of filthy Sodom. If God would save a man He must fetch him out from the world; he cannot remain part and parcel of an ungodly world and yet be God's elect one, for this is the

Lord's own word to the enemy at the gates of Eden—"I will put enmity between thee and the woman, between thy seed and her seed."

Did He not also say to Pharaoh, "I will put a division between my people and thy people"? The Lord will sooner burn all Sodom down than Lot shall continue to be associated with its crimes, and dragged down by its evil spirit. And so it came to pass that Lot was forced out; he was placed in such a strait that he must either run for his life or perish in the general burning. Happy had it been for him if he had lived all the while in the holy seclusion of Abraham; he would not then have lost the inheritance for his seed, nor have passed away under a dark, defiling cloud, nor have missed his place among the heroes of faith, of whom Paul writes in the famous chapter of the Hebrews: "These all died in faith, not having received the promises, but having seen them afar off, and were persuaded of them, and embraced them, and confessed that they were strangers and pilgrims on the earth."

Here I must pause, or you will think that I have misread my text, and that I am preaching from the words—"Remember Lot"; and, indeed, I might profitably do so, for there is much of warning in the history of Lot himself. If Christian men are so unwise as to conform themselves to the world, even if they keep up the Christian character in a measure, they will gain nothing by worldly association but being vexed with the conversation of the ungodly, and they will be great losers in their own souls: their character will be tarnished, their whole tone of feeling will be lowered, and they themselves will be wretchedly weak and unhappy. Conformity to the world is sure to end badly sooner or later: to the man himself it is injurious, and to his family ruinous.

But the text says, "Remember Lot's *wife*," and therefore I must let the husband go, and call your attention to her who, in this case, is "his worse half." When the time for separation arrived Lot's wife could not tear herself away from the world. She had always been in it, and had loved it, and delighted in it; and, though associated with a gracious man, when the time came for decision she betrayed her true character. Flight without so much as looking back was demanded of her, but this was too much; she did look back, and thus proved that she had sufficient presumption in her heart to defy God's command, and risk her all, to give a lingering love-glance at the condemned and guilty world. By that glance she perished. That is the subject of our discourse. The love of the world is death. Those who cling to sin must perish, be they who they may.

Do not fail to notice the connection of the text, for therein our Lord bids us hold the world with a loose hand, and be ever ready to leave it all. When we are called to it we are to be ready to go forth without a particle in our hands. "In that day, he which shall be upon the housetop, and his stuff in the house, let him not come down to take it away: and he that is in the field, let him likewise not return back." Life itself they were not to hold dear, but to be ready to lay it down for His sake; for He said, "Whosoever shall seek to save his life shall lose it; and whosoever shall lose his life shall preserve it."

To be divided from the world, its possessions, its maxims, its motives, is the mark of a disciple of Christ, and, in order to keep up the feeling of separateness among His followers, our Lord bade them "Remember Lot's wife." She is to be a caution to us all, for God will deal with us as with her if we sin as she did. "The thing which has been is the thing which shall be": if our hearts are glued to the world we shall perish with the world; if our desires and delights look that way, and if we find our comfort in it, we shall have to see our all consumed, and shall be ourselves consumed with it in the day of the Lord's anger. Separation is the only way of escape: we must flee from the world or perish with it. "Depart ye, depart ye, go ye out from thence, touch no unclean thing; go ye out of the midst of her; be ye clean, that bear the vessels of the Lord." I. "Remember Lot's wife": and our first call shall be—

Remember That She Was Lot's Wife

She was the wife of a man who, with all his faults, was a righteous man. She was *united to him in the closest possible bonds*, and yet she perished. She had dwelt in tents with holy Abraham, and seemed to be a sharer in all the privileges of the separated people, and yet she perished. She was dear to one who had been dear to the father of the faithful, and yet for all that she perished in her sin. This note of warning we would strike very loudly, for, commonplace as the truth is, it needs often to be repeated that ties of blood are no guarantees of grace. You may be the wife of the saintliest man of God and yet be a daughter of Belial; or you may be the husband of one of the King's daughters and yet be yourself a castaway. You may be the child of a prophet and yet the curse of a most gracious family and yet still be an alien to the commonwealth of Israel.

No earthly relationship can possibly help us if we are personally destitute of the spiritual life. Our first birth does not avail us in the kingdom of God, for that which is born of the flesh at its very best is flesh, and is prone to sin, and will certainly perish. We must be born again, for only the new birth, which is of the Spirit and from above, will bring us into covenant bonds. O children of godly parents, I beseech you look to yourselves that ye be not driven down to hell from your mother's side. O relatives of those who are the favorites of heaven, I beseech you look to yourselves that you die not within sight of heaven, in spite of all your advantages. In this matter remember Lot's wife.

Being Lot's wife, remember that she had since her marriage *shared with Lot in his journeys and adventures and trials*. We cannot tell exactly when she became Lot's wife, but we incline to the belief that it was after he had left Haran, for when Abraham left Haran we read that he took "Sarai his wife, and Lot his brother's son," but we do not read of Lot's wife. The name of Abraham's wife is given, but of Lot's wife there is no mention whatever. Again, we read, "Abram went up out of Egypt, he, and his wife, and all that he had, and Lot with him, into the south." "And Lot also, which went with Abram, had flocks, and herds, and tents," but nothing is said about his having a wife. She must have been a person of very small consideration, for even when it is certain that Lot was married, when he was taken captive and afterward rescued by Abraham, all we find is this: "And Abraham brought back all the goods, and also brought again his brother Lot, and his goods, and the women also, and the people." We suppose that Lot's wife is included under the word "the women."

Now the Holy Spirit never puts a slight under good women: in connection with their husbands they are generally mentioned with honor, and in this book of Genesis it is specially so. Sarah and Rebekah and Rachel have each an honorable memorial, and as no mention is made of Lot's wife we may infer that she was not worthy to be mentioned. She could hardly have been an inhabitant of Sodom, as the Jewish traditions assert, unless she was a widow, as they say, and the daughters mentioned were hers by a previous marriage, for at the destruction of Sodom Lot had marriageable daughters, and it would not seem that Lot had then been separated from Abraham for many years.

True, the women of Sodom may have been given in marriage at an earlier age than was usual with the Abrahamic stock, and, if so, Lot's wife may have been a native of Sodom, for it is possible that he dwelt there for twenty years. More probably, however, either in Canaan or in Egypt, Lot married a Canaanite or an Egyptian woman, a person utterly unworthy to be taken into the holy household, and therefore the marriage is not recorded.

It was the custom of that elect and separated family, as you know, to send back to Padan-aram, to fetch from thence some daughter of the same house, that the pure stock might be preserved, and that there might be no connection with the heathen. It was Abraham's desire for Isaac, and he charged his steward to carry it out, saying, "And I will make thee swear by the Lord, the God of heaven, and the God of the whole earth, that thou shalt not take a wife unto my own son of the daughters of the Canaanites, among whom I dwell: but thou shalt go unto my country, and to my kindred, and take a wife unto my Isaac." This also was Isaac's desire for Jacob, for we read, "And Isaac called Jacob, and blessed him, and charged him, and said unto him, Thou shalt not take a wife of the daughters of Canaan. Arise, go to Padan-aram, to the house of Bethuel thy mother's father; and take thee a wife from thence of the daughters of Laban thy mother's brother.

It seems to me that Lot had married a heathen woman, and so her name is omitted. Whether it be so or no, it is certain that she had shared with Lot in the capture of the city of Sodom; she had seen the ruthless sword slay the inhabitants, and she herself with her husband had been among the captives, and she had been delivered by the good sword of Abraham. So that she had been a partaker of her husband's trials and deliverances and yet she was lost.

It will be a sad, sad thing if there should come an eternal severance between those united by marriage bonds: that we should live together, and work together, and suffer together, and should be delivered by the providence of God many a time together, and should see our children grow up together, and yet should be torn apart at the last never to meet again: this is a prospect which we dare not think upon. Tremble, you whose love is not in Christ, for your union will have an end. What does the Savior say? "I tell you, in that night there shall be two in one bed; the one shall be taken, and the other shall be left. Two women shall be grinding together; the one shall be taken, and the other left. Two men shall be in the field; the one shall be taken, and the other left." It does not matter how close the association, the unbeliever must be divided from the living child of God. If you cling to the world and cast your eye back upon it you must perish in your sin, notwithstanding that you have eaten and drunk with the people of God, and have been as near to them in relationship as wife to husband, or child to parent. This makes the remembrance of Lot's wife a very solemn thing to those who are allied by ties of kindred to the people of God.

Lot's wife had also *shared her husband's privileges.* Her husband had not forgotten his association with Abraham, and he could not have failed to communicate his knowledge to her. The one God was worshiped, and Lot's wife was present. She knew of the gracious covenant which God had made with His separated people, and she knew that her husband was one of the family. She had cast in her lot with the chosen people of God apparently, though her heart was not in it, and she therefore joined their sacred song and their holy prayer. She saw the daily provision which God made for His people, and the joy which Abraham had in abiding under the shadow of the Almighty. Even in Sodom her husband kept up such separateness as he could in such an evil place, and she saw the goodness of the man with all his mistakes. When Sodom must be destroyed the angels came to their house, and she herself helped to entertain them. She received the merciful warning to escape as well as her husband, and she was urged as much as he to flee from the wrath so near at hand.

Thus is it with many of you who are enjoying all sorts of Christian privileges and are yet unsaved. You come to the Lord's table, and eat and drink of the memorials of His body and blood, and yet you remain unsaved. You seem to be part and parcel of the church of God, and if there is any privilege or advantage a share of it is set before you, if there is any fellowship you are not excluded, if there is any joy it is not denied you. You will have to say at last, "Lord, Lord, we have eaten and drunk in thy

presence, and thou hast taught in our streets," and, oh, how wretched it will
be to hear Him say, "I never knew you; depart from me, ye workers of
iniquity." It must be so if your souls are clinging to sin, and you are casting a wistful eye to the ungodly world. It must be so, and if you want a
proof—"remember Lot's wife."

Lot's wife had *shared in her husband's errors*. It was a great mistake
on his part to abandon the outwardly separated life, but she had kept to him
in it, and perhaps was the cause of his so doing. I suppose he thought he
could live above the world spiritually, and yet mingle with its votaries,
even as some now do who enter into worldly company and yet hope to
walk with God in spirit. He said to himself, "It is very uncomfortable to
wander alone in this deserted wilderness, and to dwell in these temporary
tents, I wish I had a more abiding dwelling, and could mingle on peaceable
terms with those around me." He ceased to look for the city which has
foundations whose builder and maker is God, and he wanted to take up cit-
izenship here. I should not wonder if Lot's wife influenced him in that way.
He was a man of weak mind, and while his uncle had him under his wing
he was right enough, except that even then he had what a writer calls "a
lean-to religion"; he did not stand alone, but leaned upon Abraham.

When he was married it is probable that his wife assumed the ruling
place, and guided the way of his life. She began to think that it was a pity
that the family should live in such separation, so unfashionable, so rigid,
and peculiar, and all that. She tossed her head, and cried, "Really, people
must mix with society, and not keep up old-fashioned, strait-laced
ways. You might as well be dead as be shut out from life." When her husband had an opportunity of getting out of that rigid style by leaving his
uncle she said she would like to go down Sodom way, because it would be
nice for the girls, and give them a taste of something liberal and refined.

She felt the old style was all very well for such an antiquated couple as
Abraham and Sarah, but Lot and herself belonged to a younger generation,
and were bound to get into a little society, and find eligible matches for their
young people. It would be well for them to dress better than they could learn
to do if they always kept roaming about like gypsies. You see, Abraham's
people did not study the fashions at all, and were a very vulgar sort of shepherds, who had no ideas of refinement and politeness, and it was a pity that
people in Lot's station in life should always associate with mere sheep-shear-
ers, and drovers, and the like. If they got to Sodom there would be nice
parties, and dances, and all sorts of things. Of course the people were a little loose, and rather fast; they went to plays where modesty was shocked, and
gathered in admiration around performers whose lives were openly wanton;
but then you see one must be fashionable, and wink at a good deal: we cannot expect all people to be saints, and no doubt they have their good points.

By some such talk Mistress Lot won her husband over to her way of thinking. They did not mean actually to go into the worst society of Sodom, but they intended to make a careful selection, and go only a little way. Surely they could be trusted to know where to stop. So they pitched the tent toward Sodom, where it was within an easy walk of the town, a little separated, but not far. If anything did happen that was very bad they could move away, and no harm would be done, but until they saw the harm of it they liked the neighborhood and the ways of the townsfolk. It was no doubt wise, they said, to go and see Sodom and know the people, for it would be ridiculous to condemn what they had not seen; they would therefore try it, and give the young people some idea of what the world was like.

Very sweet the city life became. The free and easy ways of Sodom came to be enjoyable. Not the gross part of Sodom life, that Lot could not bear, and it made Mistress Lot uncomfortable at times, but the liberal spirit, the fine free bearing of the people, their gaiety and artistic culture, were quite to her mind; and so she was right glad when her husband put away the old tent, had a sale of the sheep, and lived as a retired rancher in the west end of the city.

I think I am not mistaken in the conjecture that Mistress Lot's influence brought her husband there, and when there introduced him to the best families, and found suitors for the daughters, who had been fully imbued with the liberal ideas of the place. At any rate, whatever were his faults she was a partaker in them: she was with him in choosing the plain of Jordan, with him in pitching their tent toward Sodom, with him in actually settling in Sodom, and I could almost hope with him in bearing as good a protest as they could against the vilest of Sodom's sins, but certainly with him in giving up the strictness and severity of the separated life. Yet at last she was separated to him, did not utterly destroy the life of God in his soul; as for her, she never had any spiritual life, and now, when she is called to leave Sodom, she shows her love to it by a distinct disobedience of God, and an open turning to the doomed city, and so she perishes.

Oh, you who are Christian people because your friends are Christian people, you who associate with us because it happens to be the way in which you were brought up, the time will come when the secret attachment of your hearts toward a giddy world will show itself most clearly, and in a fatal moment you will give a love look toward sin which will prove you do not belong to the people of God. Then will it happen to you according to the word of the apostle, "It had been better for them not to have known the way of righteousness, than, after they known it, to turn from the holy commandment delivered unto them." II. And now, secondly, "Remember Lot's wife," and recollect that—

She Went Some Way Toward Being Saved

Mistress Lot so far believed the message that came to her about the destruction of the city that she was aroused. She rose early as her husband did, and she prepared to leave the house. She ran down the streets, she passed the city gate, she reached the open plain along with her husband. She was willing for awhile to run with him, following his example; she did so for a considerable distance, till she began to think over what she was doing, and to consider what she was leaving, and then she slackened her pace and lingered behind. Remember, then, that she did go part of the way toward safety, and yet she perished: and so many may go part of the way toward Christ, and they may go a little way out of the world, but if their hearts still linger with the ungodly they will perish notwithstanding all. There is one very solemn thought, and that is, that the angels' hand had pressed her wrist. When they said, "Up, get you gone," and Lot lingered—the men laid hold upon his hand, and the hand of his wife. So it is expressly said. An angel's hand had pressed her wrist to draw her forth to safety, and she had gone a little way under that sacred constraint; and yet she perished. Some of you may have had spiritual touches upon the conscience and heart, which you will never quite be able to forget, and the responsibility of this will cling to you, though you have drawn back from godliness and your heart cries for vanity, and lusts after its idols.

This woman was actually out of Sodom, and she was almost in Zoar, the refuge city, and yet she perished. How near she was to the little city of escape I cannot tell, but she was certainly almost there, and yet she perished. *Almost saved, but not quite.* Let me repeat those words, for they describe some of you who are present at this hour, and they may be your epitaph if you do not mind what you are about: "ALMOST SAVED, BUT NOT QUITE." Escaped from the vilest form of sin, but not truly in Christ; the mind not weaned from its idols, iniquity not given up in the soul, though perhaps given up in outward deed. O you who are *almost saved, but not quite*, "Remember Lot's wife." III. This brings me to a third point of remembrance, which is this: remember that though she went some way toward escape

She Did Actually Perish Through Sin

The first sin that she committed was that *she lingered behind*. Moses tells us "Lot's wife looked back from behind him." That is, the good old man was making such haste as he could; but she, though she had run with him side by side, lingered in the rear—I should not wonder but what the same angel had one of them by the right hand and the other by the left, while the other angel brought the two daughters on behind, but Lot's wife after all slackened her pace and fell behind. That is the first sin with most people who profess religion, but are not true to God: they begin to backslide by creeping along very slowly, they are not half so earnest as they used to be, they lag behind, One service a day is sufficient, a very little reading of the Bible contents them; they do not quite give up the appearance of prayer, but still there is very little of it; they do not see the good of being in such a fury over religion; they do not see why they should exercise any sacred violence to take the kingdom by force. They linger. It is because after all the world is master of their hearts; they would if they dare be as worldly and as ungodly as others, and they prove their true character by slackening their pace.

Having slackened her pace, the next thing she did was *she disbelieved what had been told her.* You must remember that their flight out of Sodom was to be an act of faith; for the angel said, "Look not behind thee." That Sodom was to be destroyed did not appear at all likely, for it was a bright morning. They were to fly with as much haste as if they could see the fire-shower falling, but they were not to see it; their flight was to be urged forward by faith in the angels' words. Faith may be as well exhibited by not looking as by looking. Faith is a look at Christ, but faith is a not looking at the things which are behind. Lot's wife saw the faith is a not looking at the things which are behind. Lot's wife saw the sun rising, so we are told: "the sun had risen upon the earth when Lot entered into Zoar." She saw the bright dawning and everything lit up with it, and it came across her mind—"It cannot be true, the city is not being destroyed. What a lovely morning! Why are we thus running away from house, and goods, and friends, and everything else on such a bright, clear morning as this?"

She did not truly believe, there was no real faith in her heart, and therefore she disobeyed the law of her safety and turned her face toward Sodom. Yet, mark you, she had received the angels in her house, she had seen them blind the wicked mob around her door, she had heard their majestic words of persuasion, and felt their kind compulsion: she had plenty of evidence that God was speaking but she doubted the truth of His word, and here was the very essence of her sin. What if some of you who have mingled with the godly, and have been numbered with them, and have participated in their worship, should, nevertheless, come short because of unbelief! It is by no means improbable, for out of all that came out of Egypt there were only two who entered into Canaan. They could not enter in because of unbelief; their carcasses fell in the wilderness. May it never come to pass with any of us that we shall leave our carcasses outside of the eternal hope because we, too, do not believe in Him who is invisible, but must needs walk according to the sight of the eyes.

Having come so far as lingering and doubting, her next movement was a direct act of rebellion—she turned her head: she was bidden not to look but *she dared to look.* Rebellion is as much seen in the breach of what appears to be a little command as in the violation of a great precept. Our fall at the first came by a look! Take care of little things. There is life in a look, and here is a case in which there was death in a look. She looked, but why did she look? I suppose it was this: her heart was that way. She loved

Sodom; and the separated life she abhorred. She had led her husband and her children away from the peculiar people of God, for she felt that she would rather mix with the reprobate multitude than with the chosen few. She was not of the spirit that could walk with God alone, she clung to society and to sin. Though she was running for her life she thought of her household stuff, and of the ease of Sodom, and she looked back with a lingering eye because she wanted to be there; and it came to this, that as her eye went back her whole body would have gone back if time had been allowed. She already lingered, she would soon have turned.

That one glance betrayed which way her soul was going: a little thing in professors may show what they are, and we may readily betray the inward turning of the soul by an act as simple as that of turning the neck to look toward Sodom. This was her sin.

Now, dear friends, let us remember Lot's wife each one of us by learning a personal lesson. Here is a hard thing; we must go without the camp, or utterly fail. Can you maintain the life of God and walk with Christ, and be separate from the world? Many of you cannot; you may pretend to do so, but you cannot, it is beyond you. I fear that the number of true Christians in the world is very much less than we suppose. We are encumbered with a host of people who call themselves Christians, but are as much of the world as other people, whose inheritance is in the world, whose pleasure is in the world, whose speech is worldly, and who are altogether of the world; and because they are of the world the world loves its own; and therefore there is little or no strife between them and the world. Alas, I fear the church is not true to itself, and therefore the world begins to love it. It says, "You have come to live with us, and do as we do, and you do not bear your awkward protests as you used to do, and so we need not to burn you as we did your fathers. You are hail fellow, well met! with us, and therefore we will treat you kindly." Only let us live as Christ lived, and we shall find the dogs of this world howling at us as they used to do at our forefathers.

My hearers, can you live the separated life? If you can, God help you and bless you in it, but if you cannot, recollect though you do not so go into Sodom as to indulge in its grosser sins, yet the very looking at it, the wishing for it, the desiring to be there shows where your heart is, and your heart's tendency is your true character. You will be judged according to the going of your heart. If your heart goes toward the mountain to escape, and if you hasten to be away with Christ to be His separated follower, you shall be saved: but if your heart still goes after evil and sin, his servants you are whom you obey, and from your evil master you shall get your black reward.

IV. Here comes our remembrance of Lot's wife in the fourth and most solemn place, and that is—remember that

Her Doom Was Terrible

"Remember Lot's wife." Remember that she perished with the same doom as that which happened to the inhabitants of Sodom and Gomorrah, *but that doom befell her at the gates of Zoar.* Oh, if I must be damned, let it be with the mass of the ungodly, having always been one of them; but to get up to the very gates of heaven, and to perish there, will be a most awful thing!

To have lived with God's people, to have been numbered with them, to have been joined to them by ties of blood, and then after all to perish, will be horrible indeed! To have heard the gospel, to have felt the gospel, too, in a measure, to have amended one's life because of it, to have escaped from the filthiest corruption of the world, and to have become moral, and amiable, and excellent, and yet still not to have been weaned from the world, not to have been clean divorced from sin, and so to perish—the thought is intolerable. That same brine and brimstone which fell upon the inhabitants of the four cities overtook Lot's wife. She was on the margin of the shower, and as it fell she was salted with fire, she was turned into a pillar of salt where she stood. Dreadful doom! On the verge of mercy to be slain by justice; on the brink of salvation to be the victim of eternal wrath!

This came upon her of a *sudden*, too. What a picture! She stops as she is flying, she turns her head! She scarcely looks! The gaze is not long enough to single out her own house—and, lo, she is turned into a pillar! The fire-salt has fallen on her! She will never move again! She had not time to start or turn, and, with her neck just as it was, she stands as a statue of salt, a warning to all who should pass that way. I do not suppose Lot's wife to be standing there now, as some travelers have imagined: the pillar was not even there in Christ's day, for if it had been, as Bengel very properly remarks, our Lord would have said, "See Lot's wife"; but as she was not there he said, "Remember" her. Her doom came on a sudden, without a further warning or a moment's time to consider.

What if sudden death should strike some of you down at this moment? You professors who still love the world, what if you now fell dead? You professed Christians who sneak in among the ungodly to have a suck at their pleasures, suppose you should be struck down in the theater one of these days! You who pretend to be Christians and frequent the dancing saloon, suppose you should fall dead there! It would not be a new thing under the sun, for God deals severely with those who profess to come under His covenant; He has jealous laws for those who join His church and yet have not the grace of God in their hearts. These die not the death of common men, but are often overtaken by strange punishments, that the world may see that the Lord has set a wall of fire around His church, which none may break through on peril of their lives.

Ananias and Sapphira entered the church, but they could not live there; a glance of Peter's eye and they fell dead before him. Such judgments still purge the ranks of the professing church, as all that observe must know, for the Lord will be sanctified of them who come near to Him. "For this cause," says the apostle, "Some are sickly among you, and many sleep," because the discipline of God goes on in the midst of His visible church. He lets the world alone till the fire-shower comes, but to those who profess to be His people He is always a jealous God. I speak strong things; strong things are wanted in these compromising days. May the Holy Spirit impress these weighty facts on all your hearts.

The worst point, perhaps, about the perishing of Lot's wife lay in this, that *she perished in the very act of sin*, and had no space for repentance given her. In the instant she turned her head she was a pillar of salt. It is a dreadful thing to die in the very act of sin, to be caught away by the justice of God while the transgression is being perpetrated. Yet such a thing may happen, and let those who profess to be Christians and yet parley with sin "remember Lot's wife," and how swift God is to deal out His judgment against professors who betray His holy name and cause.

Remember Lot

I cannot help going back to the text I started with, which was one of my own making, and that is, "Remember Lot." Though Lot himself was a righteous man and escaped from the doom of the wicked city, yet I cannot help tracing the death of Lot's wife in some degree to her husband. When a man walks with God and imitates God he gets to be a great character—that is Abraham. When a man walks with a holy man and imitates *him* he may rise to be a good character, but he will be a weak one—that is Lot. But when one walks with Lot, the weak character, and only copies him, the result will be a failure—that is Lot's wife. It is like the boy's copy book. If he will copy the top line the boy makes an Abraham line; but if the next time he does not look at the top line, but imitates the second—that makes a Lot line, very far short of the first. If he next copies No. 3, the Lot line, the result will be poor affair—that is Lot's wife.

Beloved, we are to live having the perfect Father for our example, look-ing and following in His steps, and if we do so by the power of the Spirit we shall reach a grand noble, Abrahamic character. But suppose you get to imitate some good man, and he is your standard, you will make a sec-ond-rate Christian, it will be a weak affair, like Lot. And then if your wife and children get copying *you*, oh, the mischief that must come of it!

Lot ought to have been more firm, more steadfast, more thorough. He had no business to have gone to Sodom. If he had said to his wife, "No, my wife, we belong to a chosen people. God called us out of Haran, and away from the gods of our fathers, that we might live a separated life, and here I am going to stop, and you must stop with me," she would have had to obey, or even if she had not done so, Lot was not to do evil to please his wife. She could not have learned the ways of Sodom—she might have given her heart still to the world, but she could not have been so clearly mixed up with it, and her daughters could not have been so lacking in morality as they were if he had resolved to live apart from the town's people.

I believe that fathers and husbands ought to take the lead in the management of their families, and parents are bound to arrange their households after a godly fashion. Do not say, "Oh, we cannot manage our families." You must do it. Eli failed in this, and, instead of being firm, he timidly said, "Do not so, my sons." Poor dear old Eli, he did not like to get into trouble with his sons by finding fault with them. But what did his softness cost him? The Lord struck down his family because he had not ordered his household aright. If Christian men leave their families to go anyhow they choose, they will soon find the Lord has a controversy with them; and if the children and if the wife should after all perish, it will be a horrible thought for the head of the household, even if he be a saved man, that it was his ill example which caused their ruin.

It was partly Lot's own doing that his wife became what she was. If Lot had never gone to Sodom his wife would not have perished near it. Look to yourselves lest you lead others astray. Keep near to God and you will be blessed and become a blessing to others. Abraham did not have this trouble with Sarah, nor Isaac with Rebekah, for they walked with God, and their influence was felt in their tents. Live near to God, and let your own life be according to the command which God gave the patriarch—"Walk with me and be perfect," and you shall see that He will bless your household, and your children after you; but if you do not thus walk before the Lord you will have to "remember Lot's wife." May God add His blessing to these words, for Jesus' sake. Amen.

7

Manoah's Wife and Her Excellent Argument[*]

And Manoah said unto his wife, We shall surely die, because we have seen God. But his wife said unto him, If the Lord were pleased to kill us, he would not have received a burnt offering and a meat-offering at our hands, neither would he have shewed us all these things, nor would as at this time have told us such things as these (Judges 12:22–23).

The first remark arising out of the story of Manoah and his wife is this—that *oftentimes we pray for blessings which will make us tremble when we receive them.* Manoah had asked that he might see the angel, and he saw him: in answer to his request the wonderful One condescended to reveal Himself a second time, but the consequence was that the good man was filled with astonishment and dismay, and turning to his wife, he exclaimed, "We shall surely die because we have seen God."

Beloved, do we always know what we are asking for when we pray? We are imploring an undoubted blessing, and yet if we knew the way in which such blessing must necessarily come, we should, perhaps, hesitate before we pressed our cause. You have been entreating very much for growth in holiness. Do you know that in almost every case that means increased affliction? For we do not make much progress in the divine life except when the Lord is pleased to try us in the furnace and purge us with many fires. Do you desire the mercy on that condition? Are you willing to take it as God pleases to send it, and to say, "Lord, if spiritual growth implies trial, if it signifies a long sickness of body, if it means deep depression of soul, if it entails the loss of property, if it involves the taking away of my dearest friends, yet I make no reserve, but include in the prayer all

* This sermon is taken from The Metropolitan Tabernacle Pulpit and was preached at the Metropolitan Tabernacle, Newington, in 1887.

that is needful to the good end. When I say, sanctify me wholly, spirit, soul, and body, I leave the process to your discretion?"

Suppose you really knew all that it would bring upon you, would you not pray, at any rate, with more solemn tones? I hope you would not hesitate, but, counting all the cost, would still desire to be delivered from sin; but, at any rate, you would put up your petition with deliberation, weighing every syllable, and then when the answer came you would not be so astonished at its peculiar form. Often and often the blessing which we used so eagerly to *im*plore is the occasion of the suffering which we *de*plore. We do not know God's methods. We set Him ways which He does not choose to follow, even as John Newton confessed to have done when he asked that he might grow in grace. He says—

> I hoped that in some favored hour,
> At once He'd answer my request,
> And, by His love's constraining power
> Subdue my sins and give me rest.
>
> Instead of this, He made me feel
> The hidden evils of my heart;
> And let the angry powers of hell
> Assault my soul in every part.
>
> Yea, more, with His own hand He seemed
> Intent to aggravate my woe;
> Crossed all the fair designs I schemed,
> Blasted my gourds, and laid me low.

This is the Lord's way of answering prayer for faith and grace. He comes with rods of chastisement, and makes us suffer for our follies, for thus alone can He deliver our childish spirits from them. He comes with sharp ploughshares and tears up the soul, for thus only can we be made to yield Him a harvest. He comes with hot irons and burns us to the heart; and when we inquire, "Why all this?" the answer comes to us, "This is what you asked for, this is the way in which the Lord answers your requests." Perhaps, at this moment, the fainting feeling that some of you are now experiencing, which makes you fear that you will surely die, may be accounted for by your own prayers. I should like you to look at your present sorrows in that light, and say, "After all, I can see that now my God has given to me exactly what I sought at His hands. I asked to see the angel, and I have seen Him, and now it is that my spirit is cast down within me."

A Second remark is this—*Very frequently deep prostration of spirit is the forerunner of some remarkable blessing.* It was to Manoah and to his wife the highest conceivable joy of life, the climax of their ambition, that they should be the parents of a son by whom the Lord should begin to deliver Israel. Joy filled them—inexpressible joy—at the thought of it; but, at the time when the good news was first communicated, Manoah, at least, was made so heavy in spirit that he said, "We shall surely die, for we have seen an angel of the Lord."

Take it as a general rule that dull skies foretell a shower of mercy. Expect sweet favor when you experience sharp affliction. When God's great wagons loaded down with blessings are coming to your door, you will full often hear beforehand the wheels rolling and rumbling horridly. You will think that it is the death-cart, perhaps, although it is your Father's treasure that is coming to your door.

Do you not remember, concerning the apostles, that they feared as they entered into the cloud on Mount Tabor? And yet it was in that cloud that they saw their Master transfigured; and you and I have had many a fear about the cloud we were entering, although we were therein to see more of Christ and His glory than we had ever beheld before. The cloud which you fear makes the external wall of that secret chamber wherein the Lord reveals Himself. It is the thick veil which seems to shut out the light of day, but as we pass behind it into what seems the thick darkness we behold the bright light of the shekinah of God's presence shining above the mercy seat. Trials come before comforts, like John the Baptist with his rough garment before Jesus the consolation of Israel. Be therefore of good cheer.

Blessed be God for rough winds. They have blown home many a barque which else had sailed to destruction. Blessed be God for trial; it has been Christ's black dog to fetch in many a sheep which else had wandered into the wolf's jaws. Blessed be our Master for the fire: it has burnt away the dross. Blessed be our Master for the file: it has taken off the rust. Not in themselves considered are these things blessings, but they are often overruled to be so by the mighty hand of God, and they are frequently the harbingers of great favors yet to come.

Before you can carry Samson in your arms, Manoah, you must be made to say, "We shall surely die." Before the minister shall preach the word to thousands, he must be emptied and made to tremble under a sense of inability. Before the Sunday school teacher shall bring her girls to Christ, she shall be led to see how weak and insufficient she is. I do believe that whenever the Lord is about to use us in His household, He takes us like a dish and wipes us right out and sets us on the shelf, and then afterward He takes us down and puts thereon His own heavenly meat, with which to fill the souls of others. There must as a rule be an emptying, a turning upside down, and a putting on one side, before the very greatest blessing comes. Manoah felt that he must die, and yet die he could not, for he was to be the father of Samson, the deliverer of Israel and the terror of Philistia.

Let me offer a third remark, which is this—*great faith is in many instances subject to fits.* What great faith Manoah had! His wife was barren, yet when she was told by the angel that she should bear a child, he believed it, although no heavenly messenger had come to himself personally—so believed it that he did not want to see the man of God a second time to be told that it would be so, but only to be informed how to bring up the child: that was all. "Well," says old Bishop Hall, "might he be the father of strong Samson, that had such a strong faith." He had a strong faith indeed, and yet here he is saying in alarm, "We shall surely die, because we have seen God."

Do not judge a man by any solitary word or act, for if you do you will surely mistake him. Cowards are occasionally brave, and the bravest men are sometimes cowards; and there are men who would be worse cowards practically if they were a little less cowardly than they are. A man may be too much a coward to confess that he is timid. Trembling Manoah was so outspoken, honest, and sincere that he expressed his feelings, which a more politic person might have concealed. Though fully believing what had been spoken from God, yet at the same time this doubt was on him, as the result of his belief in tradition: "We shall surely die, because we have seen God."

You know how many parallel cases there are in Scripture to this. Look at majestic Abraham, the very father of the faithful—a prince, I might call him, among believers; and yet he denies his wife, and says, "She is my sister." These things do not prove that he had no faith: they only show that the strongest faith is mixed with unbelief, and that the best of men are men at the best.

So, too, with mighty Elijah. When you see him on the top of Carmel pleading there with God, and bringing down the fire, and when you hear him cry, "Take the prophets of Baal: let not one escape," and observe that man of iron, slaying them all at the foot of the hill, why you cannot believe it possible that he is the same trembler who flees from the face of Jezebel, and sits down under one of the desert junipers, and cries, "Let me die: I am no better than my fathers." But it is so. It is ever so. God's saints generally show their weakness in the very grace wherein their strength lies, and this great believer, Manoah, is troubled with a miserable attack of doubt, which so masters him that he expects sudden death.

Now, have any of you lately had such a fit as that upon you? Well, dear friend, do not indulge it. Let it be a fit, and let it come to an end, as no doubt it did with Manoah. He did not continue long in his fainting condition, but it was bad while it lasted. It is very bad when persons have fits every day, and worse still if they are always in fits. It will not do for us to begin to make excuses for our unbelief, or to allow ourselves to remain in depression of spirit. Our soul must not be suffered to lie cleaving to the dust. We must catechize our hearts, and say, "Why are you cast down, O my soul? Why are you disquieted within me? Hope in God, for I shall yet praise Him who is the health of my countenance and my God."

Yet do not be surprised, or write your own condemnation, as though some strange thing had befallen you, for so has it happened unto others, that though they have been strong in faith they have had strong misgivings at times.

Once again, another remark is that *it is a great mercy to have a Christian companion to go to for counsel and comfort whenever your soul is depressed.* Manoah had married a capital wife. She was the better one of the two in sound judgment. She was the weaker vessel by nature, but she was the stronger-believer, and probably that was why the angel was sent to her, for the angels are best pleased to speak with those who have faith, and if they have the pick of their company, and the wife has more faith than the husband, they will visit the wife sooner than her spouse, for they love to take God's messages to those who will receive them with confidence. She was full of faith, evidently, and so when her husband tremblingly said, "We shall surely die," she did not believe in such a mistrustful inference. Moreover, though some say that women cannot reason, yet here was a woman whose arguments were logical and overwhelming. Certain it is that women's perceptions are generally far clearer than men's reasonings: they look at once into a truth, while we are hunting for our spectacles. Their instincts are generally as safe as our reasonings, and therefore when they have in addition a clear logical mind they make the wisest of counselors.

Well, Manoah's wife not only had clear perceptions, but she had capital reasoning faculties. She argued, according to the language of the text, that it was not possible that God should kill them after what they had seen and heard. O that every man had such a prudent, gracious wife as Manoah had! O that whenever a man is cast down a Christian brother or sister stood ready to cheer him with some reminder of the Lord's past goodness, or with some gracious promise from the divine word. It may happen to be the husband who cheers the wife, and in such a case it is equally beautiful. We have known a Christian sister to be very nervous and very often depressed and troubled: what a mercy to her to have a Christian husband whose strength of faith can encourage her to smile away her griefs, by resting in the everlasting faithfulness and goodness of the Lord. How careful ought young people to be in choosing their partners in life! When two horses pull together how smoothly and the chariot runs; but if one horse draws one way and the other pulls in the opposite direction, what trouble there is sure to be.

Suppose Manoah had happened to have an unbelieving wife. Ah, Manoah, how your spirit would have gone down, down, down into despair, till you would have fulfilled your own sad prophecy. If he had been troubled with a wife like Mistress Job, and she had uttered some bitter saying just at the time when he was in anguish, how much more severe would his griefs have become. But Mistress Manoah was a believing woman, she argued out the question most discreetly, and her husband found peace again.

Tonight, as God the Holy Spirit shall help us, we will take up the argument of Manoah's wife, and see whether it will not also comfort our hearts. She had three strings to her bow, good woman. One was—The Lord does not mean to kill us, because He has accepted our sacrifices. The second was—He does not mean to kill us, or else He would not have shown us all these things. And the third was—He will not kill us, or else He would not, as at this time, have told us such things as these. So the three strings to her bow were *accepted sacrifice*, *gracious revelations*, and *precious promises*. Let us dwell upon each of them. I. And, first,

Accepted Sacrifices

I will suppose that I am addressing a brother who is sadly tried, and terribly cast down, and who therefore has begun to lament—

> The Lord has forsaken me quite;
> My God will be gracious no more.

Beloved, is that possible? Has not God of old accepted on your behalf the offering of His Son Jesus Christ? You have believed in Jesus, dear friend. You do believe in Him now. Lay your hand on your heart, and put the question solemnly to yourself, "Do you believe on the Son of God?" You are able to say, "Yes, Lord, notwithstanding all my unhappiness, I do believe in You, and rest the stress and weight of my soul's interests on Your power to save." Well, then, you have God's own word, recorded in His own infallible Book, assuring you that Jesus Christ was accepted of God on your behalf, for He laid down His life for as many as believe in Him, that they might never perish. He stood as their surety, and suffered as their substitute. Is it possible that this should be unavailing, and that after all they may be cast away? The argument of Manoah's wife was just this— "Did we not put the kid on the rock, and as we put it there was it not consumed? It was consumed instead of us; we shall not die, for the victim has been consumed. The fire will not burn us: it has spent itself upon the sacrifice. Did you not see it go up in smoke, and see the angel ascend with it? The fire is gone; it cannot fall on us to destroy us."

This being interpreted into the gospel is just this—Have we not seen the Lord Jesus Christ fastened to the cross? Have we not beheld Him in agonies extreme? Has not the fire of God consumed Him? Have we not seen Him rising, as it were, from that sacred fire in the resurrection and the ascension, to go into the glory? Because the fire of Jehovah's wrath had spent itself on Him we shall not die. He has died instead of us.

It cannot be that the Lord has made Him suffer, the just for the unjust, and now will make the believer suffer too. It cannot be that Christ loved

His church, and gave Himself for it, and that now the church must perish also. It cannot be that the Lord has laid on Him the iniquity of us all, and now will lay our iniquity on us too. It were not consistent with justice. It would nullify the vicarious sacrifice of Christ, make it a superfluity of cruelty which achieved nothing. The atonement cannot be made of none effect, the very supposition would be blasphemy.

O look, my soul, look to the Redeemer's cross, and as you see how God accepts Christ, be filled with content. Hear how the "It is finished" of Jesus on earth is echoed from the throne of God Himself, as He raises up His Son from the dead, and bestows glory upon Him. Hear this, I say, and as you hear, attend to the power of this argument—If the Lord had been pleased to kill us, He would not have accepted His Son for us. If He meant *us* to die, would He have put Him to death too? How can it be? The sacrifice of Jesus must effectually prevent the destruction of those for whom He offered up Himself as a sacrifice. Jesus dying for sinners, and yet the sinners denied mercy! Inconceivable and impossible! My soul, whatever your inward feelings and the tumult of your thoughts, the accepted sacrifice shows that God is not pleased to kill you.

But, if you notice, in the case of Manoah, they had offered a burnt-sacrifice and a meat-offering too. Well, now, in addition to the great, grand sacrifice of Christ, which is our trust, we, dear brothers and sisters, have offered other sacrifices to God, and in consequences of His acceptance of such sacrifices we cannot imagine that He intends to destroy us.

First, let me conduct your thoughts back to the offering of *prayer* which you have presented. I will speak for myself. I recall now, running over my diary mentally, full many an instance in which I have sought the Lord in prayer and He has most graciously heard me. I am as sure that my requests have been heard as ever Manoah could have been sure that his sacrifice was consumed upon the rock. May I not infer from this that the Lord does not mean to destroy me? You know that it has been so with you, dear friend. You are down in the dumps today, you are beginning to raise many questions about divine love; but there have been times—you know there have—when you have sought the Lord and He has heard you. You can say, "This poor man cried, and the Lord heard him, and delivered him from all his fears."

Perhaps you have not jotted down the fact in a book, but your memory holds the indelible record. Your soul has made her personal boast in the Lord concerning His fidelity to His promise in helping His people in the hour of need, for you have happily proved it in your own case. Now, friend, if the Lord had been pleased to kill you, would He have heard your prayers? If He had meant to cast you out after all, would He have heard you so many times? If He had sought a quarrel against you He might have had cause for that quarrel years ago, and have said to you, "When you make many prayers I will not hear." But since He has listened to your cries and tears, and many a time answered your petitions, He cannot intend to kill you.

Again, you brought to Him, years ago, not only your prayers but *yourself*. Remember that glad hour when you said,

> Now, O God, thine own I am;
> Now I give thee back thine own
> Freedom, friends, and health, and fame,
> Consecrate to thee alone;
> Thine I live, thrice happy I!
> Happier still if thine I die."

You gave yourself over to Christ, body, soul, spirit, all your goods, all your hours, all your talents, every faculty, and every possible acquirement, and you said, "Lord, I am not my own, but I am bought with a price." Now, at that time did not the Lord accept you? You have at this very moment a lively recollection of the sweet sense of acceptance you had at that time. Even now your heart sings,

> Lord in the strength of grace
> With a glad heart and free,
> Myself, my residue of days,
> I consecrate to thee.

Though you are at this time sorely troubled, yet you would not wish to withdraw from the consecration which you then made, but on the contrary you declare,

> High heaven, that heard the solemn vow,
> That vow renewed shall daily hear,
> Till, in life's latest hour, I bow,
> And bless in death a bond so dear.

Now, would the Lord have accepted the offering of yourself to Him if He meant to destroy you? Would He have let you say, "I am your servant and the son of your handmaid: you have loosed by bonds"? Would He have permitted you to declare as you can boldly assert tonight, "I bear in my body the marks of the Lord Jesus," delighting to remember the time of your baptism into Him, whereby your body, washed with His pure body, was declared to be the Lord's forever. Would He enable you to feel a joy in the very mark of your consecration, as well as in the consecration itself, if He meant to slay you? Oh, surely not! He does not let a person give himself up to Him, and then cast him away. That cannot be.

Some of us, dear friends, can recollect how, growing out of this last sacrifice, there have been others. The Lord has accepted our offerings at other times too, for our works, faith, and labors of love have been owned of His Spirit. There are some of you, I am pleased to remember, whom God has blest to the conversion of little children whom you have tried to teach for Jesus. You have some in heaven whom you brought to the Savior, and there are others on earth whom you can look upon with great joy because God was pleased to make you the instrument of their conviction and their after conversion. Some of you, I perceive, are ministers of the gospel, others of you preach at the corners of the streets, and there have been times in your lives—I am sure that you wish they were ten times as many—in which God has been pleased to bless your efforts, so that hearts have yielded to the sway of Jesus.

Now, you do not put any trust in those things, nor do you claim any merit for having served your Master, but still I think they may be thrown in as a matter of consolation, and you may say, If the Lord had meant to destroy me, would He have enabled me to preach His gospel? Would He have helped me to weep over men's souls? Would He have enabled me to gather those dear children like lambs to His bosom? Would He have granted me my longing desire to bear fruit in His vineyard, if He did not mean to bless me? Surely He will not let me be like Judas, who preached the gospel and betrayed his Master. But, having accepted me and given me joy in my work, and success in it, He will continue with me and help me even to the end. As Mr. Wesley well puts it—

> Me, if purposed to destroy
> For past unfaithfulness,
> Would God vouchsafe to employ
> And still so strangely bless?

Those are comparatively small things, but sometimes small things help our small minds. Little fishes are sweet, and little diamonds are precious, and so little evidences may let in a great deal of peace. They may at least help us while we are looking out for something better, so that we may rise out of our troubles and grasp the higher joys.

So much upon the first point. Mistress Manoah argued that, if God had accepted their offerings, He did not mean to kill them; and there is our argument tonight, for He has accepted the great sacrifice of Christ, and then He has accepted the sacrifices which His grace has enabled us to offer, and therefore He does not mean to kill us.

"Who said He did?" someone asks. Well, the devil has said that numbers of times. He is a liar from the beginning, and he does not improve a bit. He will have the impudence to say this to you when you have just been in the presence of Christ. As you come fresh from the closet he will meet you outside the door, and he will tell you that the Lord has utterly forsaken you, for there are no bounds to his falsehood. Reply to him, if he is worth replying to at all, in the language of our text. II. But now, the second argument was that they had received

Gracious Revelations

"If the Lord were pleased to kill us, he would not have shewed us all these things." Now, what has the Lord shown you, my dear friends? I will mention one or two things.

First, the Lord has shown you, perhaps years ago, or possibly at this moment He is showing you for the first time—*your sin*. What a sight that was when we first had it. Some of you never saw your sins, but your sins are there all the same. In an old house, perhaps, there is a cellar into which nobody goes, and the windows are always kept shut. There is a wooden shutter: no light ever comes in. You live in the house comfortably enough, not knowing what is there; but one day you take a candle, and go down the steps, and open that moldy door, and when it is opened, dear me! What a damp, pestilential smell! How foul the floor is! All sorts of living creatures hop away from under your feet. There are growths on the very walls—a heap of roots in the corner, sending out those long yellow growths which look like the fingers of death. And there is a spider, and there are a hundred like him, of such a size as cannot be grown, except in such horrible places. You get out as quickly as ever you can. You do not like the look of it.

Now, the candle did not make that cellar bad; the candle did not make it filthy. No, the candle only showed what there was. And when you get the carpenter to take down that shutter which you could not open anyhow, for it had not been opened for years, and when the daylight comes in, it seems more horrible than it did by candlelight, and you wonder, indeed, however you did go across it with all those dreadful things all around you, and you cannot be satisfied to live upstairs now till that cellar downstairs has been perfectly cleansed.

That is just like our heart; it is full of sin, but we do not know it. It is a den of unclean birds, a menagerie of everything that is fearful, and fierce, and furious—a little hell stocked with devils. Such is our nature; such is our heart. Now, the Lord showed me mine years ago, as He did some of you, and the result of a sight of one's heart is horrible. Well does Dr. Young say, "God spares all eyes but His own, that fearful sight, a naked human heart." Nobody ever did see all His heart as it really is. You have only seen a part, but, when seen, it is so horrible that it is enough to drive a man out of His senses to see the evil of His nature.

Now, let us gather some honey out of this dead lion. Brother, if the Lord had meant to destroy us, He would not have shown us our sin, because we were happy enough previously, were we not? In our own poor way we were content enough, and if He did not mean to pardon us, it was not like the Lord to show us our sin, and so to torment us before our time, unless

He meant to take it away. We were swine, but we were satisfied enough with the husks we ate; and why not let us remain swine? What was the good of letting us see our filthiness if He did not purpose to take it away?

It never can be possible that God sets Himself studiously to torture the human mind by making it conscious of its evil, if He never intends to supply a remedy. Oh no! A deep sense of sin will not save you, but it is a pledge that there is something begun in your soul which may lead to salvation; for the deep sense of sin does as good as say, "The Lord is laying bare the disease that He may cure it. He is letting you see the foulness of that underground cellar of your corruption, because He means to cleanse it for you." So, beloved, if the Lord had meant to kill us He would not have shown us such things as the infamy of our nature and the horror of our fall; but since He has revealed to us our nakedness and poverty He desires to clothe and enrich us.

But He has shown us more than this, for He has made us see *the hollowness and emptiness of the world.* There are some here present who, at one time, were very gratified with the pleasures and amusements of the world. The theater was a great delight to them. The ballroom afforded them supreme satisfaction. To be able to dress just after their own fancy, and to spend money on their own whims, were the very acme of delight; but there came a time when across all these the soul perceived a mysterious handwriting, which being interpreted ran thus: "Vanity of vanities; all is vanity." These very people went to the same amusements, but they seemed so dull and stupid that they came away saying, "We do not care a bit for them. The joys are all gone. What seemed gold turns out to be gilt; and what we thought marble was only white paint. The varnish is cracked, the tinsel is faded, the coloring has vanished. Mirth laughs like an idiot, and pleasure grins like madness."

I have known persons in that condition of mind seek after still more stirring pleasures. They have thought that, if they went a step farther, till what was mere amusement came to be vice, perhaps they might find something there. They have tried it, till they have drained all the cups of the devil's banquet, and found them sickening as lukewarm water, insipid, and even nauseous. Satiety has come upon them, and they have been weary of life.

Now, beloved, the Lord has taught many of us this in different ways, even those of us who have never gone very far into worldly amusement; and so we have learned that there is nothing around the spacious globe that can satisfy a hungry soul. We, too, have heard the words, "Vanity of vanities: all is vanity," sounding in our hearts; and now do you think that, if the Lord had meant to kill us, He would have taught us this? Why, no; He would have said, "Let them alone, they are given unto idols. They are only going to have one world in which they can rejoice; let them enjoy it."

He would have let the swine go on with their husks if He had not meant to turn them into His children, and bring them to His own bosom. I think I told you once of a story which illustrates this, of a good wife— a good Christian woman—who had been converted. Her husband remained a godless and licentious man. Nevertheless, her gentleness and patience were surpassing, and one night, while out in a drinking party, her husband made a boast that there was not one of them that had such a wife as he had. He said she was far too religious, but for all that there was never such a woman. "And if I were to take you now," said he, "ten of you, home to supper tonight, though it is past twelve, she would provide for you, receive you with a smile, and never say a syllable by way of complaint."

They did not believe it, and so they went down to the house. She was sitting up past midnight, weary, and the wicked husband said he had brought in his friends and he wished them to have some supper. She had to forage very carefully, and make the best of what there was in the house, and she begged the gentlemen to have a little patience and wait; the meal might not be quite served as she should like to have it, since the servants were in bed, but still she would do her best. She managed well, the company sat down at the table, the lady treated them most graciously, and the husband had won his bet.

Then they asked her how it was that she could bear with such treatment, and act so nobly. Bursting into tears, when they pressed her again and again, she answered, "I have long prayed for my dear husband, and anxiously desired his salvation, but I am afraid he never will be saved, and so I have made up my mind to make him as happy as possible while he is here, fearing he will have no happiness hereafter." Now do you not think that God would act on that principle with you and with me if He meant to leave us to perish? Would He not allow us to have the enjoyment of this world at any rate? But because He has taught us that this world is a mockery and a cheat, I gather that He will not destroy us.

But He has taught us something better than this—namely, *the preciousness of Christ.* Unless we are awfully deceived—self-deceived, I mean—we have known what it is to lose the burden of our sin at the foot of the cross. We have known what it is to see the suitability and all-sufficiency of the merit of our dear Redeemer, and we have rejoiced in Him with joy unspeakable and full of glory. If He had meant to destroy us He would not have shown us Christ.

Sometimes also we have strong desires after *God!* What pinings after communion with Him have we felt! What longings to be delivered from sin! What yearnings to be perfect! What aspirations to be with Him in heaven, and what desires to be like Him while we are here! Now these longings, cravings, desirings, yearnings, do you think the Lord would have put them into our hearts if he had meant to destroy us? What would be the good of it? Would it not, indeed, be a superfluity of cruelty thus to make us wish for what we could never have, and pine after what we should never gain? O beloved, let us be comforted about these things. If He had meant to kill us, He would not have shown us such things as these. III. I shall have no time to dwell upon the last source of comfort which is what the Lord has spoken to us—

Many Precious Promises

"Nor would he have told us such things as these." At almost any time when a child of God is depressed, if he goes to the Word of God and to prayer, and looks up, he will generally get a hold of some promise or other. I know I generally do. I could not tell you, dear friends, tonight, what promise would suit your case, but the Lord always knows how to apply the right word at the right time; and when a promise is applied with great power to the soul, and you are enabled to plead it at the mercy-seat, you may say, "If the Lord had meant to kill us He would not have made us such a promise as this." I have a promise that hangs up before my eyes whenever I awake every morning, and it has continued in its place for years. It is a stay to my soul. It is this—"I will not fail you nor forsake you." Difficulties arise, funds run short, sickness comes; but somehow or other my text always seems to flow like a fountain—"I will not fail you nor forsake you." If the Lord had meant to kill us, He would not have said that to us.

What is your promise tonight? What have you got a hold of? If you have not laid hold of any, and feel as if none belonged to you, yet there are such words as these, "This is a faithful saying and worthy of all acceptation, that Christ Jesus came into the world to save sinners," and you are one. Ah, if He had meant to destroy you, He would not have spoken a text of such a wide character on purpose to include your case. A thousand promises go down to the lowest deep into which a heart can ever descend, and if the Lord had meant to destroy a soul in the deeps, He would not have sent a gospel promise down even to that extreme.

I must finish, and therefore I should like to say these two or three words tonight to you who are unconverted, but who are troubled in your souls. You think that God means to destroy you. Now, dear friend, I take it that if the Lord had meant to kill you, He would not have sent the gospel to you. If there had been a purpose and a decree to destroy you, He would not have brought you here. I am glad to see unconverted people here on Thursday nights. When souls begin to love week-night services I always think that there is a something good in them toward the Lord God of Israel.

Now you are sitting to hear that Jesus has died to save such as you are. You are sitting where you are bidden to trust Him and be saved. If the Lord had meant to slay you I do not think He would have sent me on such a fruitless errand as to tell you of a Christ who could not save you. I think, on Thursday nights especially, I may hope that I have a picked congregation whom God intends to bless. Besides, some of you have had your lives spared very remarkably. You have been in accidents on land or on sea—perhaps in battle and shipwreck. You have been raised from a sickbed. If the Lord had meant to destroy you, surely He would have let you die then; but He has spared you, and you are getting on in years; surely it is time that you yielded to His mercy and gave yourself up into the hands of grace.

If the Lord had meant to destroy you, surely, He would not have brought you here tonight, for, possibly, I am addressing one who has come here, wondering why. All the time he has been sitting here he has been saying to himself, "I do not know how I got into this place, but here I am." God means to bless you tonight, I trust, and He will, dear friend, if you breathe this prayer of heaven—"Father, forgive me! I have sinned against heaven and before You, but for Christ's sake forgive me! I put my trust in Your Son." You shall find eternal life, rejoicing in the sacrifice which God has accepted. You shall one of these days rejoice in the revelations of His love, and in the promises which He gives you, and say as we say tonight, "If the Lord were pleased to kill us He would not have showed us all these things." The Lord bless you for Christ's sake. Amen.

8

*Ruth: Spiritual Gleaning**

Let her glean even among the sheaves, and reproach her not
(Ruth 2:15).

Our country cousins have been engaged recently in harvest occupations, and most of them understand what is meant by gleaning. Perhaps they are not all of them so wise as to understand the heavenly art of spiritual gleaning. That is the subject which I have chosen for our meditation on this occasion, my attention having been called to it while I have been riding along through the country; and as I like to improve the seasons of the year as they come and go, I shall give you a few homely remarks with regard to spiritual gleaning. In the first place, we shall observe, that there is *a great Husbandman*†. It was Boaz in this case; it is our Heavenly Father who is the Husbandman in the other case. Secondly, we shall notice *a humble gleaner*. It was Ruth in this instance; it is every believer who is represented by her; at least, we shall so consider the subject. And, in the third place, here is *a very gracious permission given*: "Let her glean even among the sheaves, and reproach her not." I. In the first place, then, we will consider something concerning

The Great Husbandman—God

The God of the whole earth is a great Husbandman; in fact, all farming operations are really dependent on Him. Man may plow the soil, and he may sow the seed, but God alone gives the increase. It is He who sends the clouds and the sunshine, it is He who directs the winds and the rain, and so, by various processes of nature, He brings forth the food for man. All the farming, however, which God does, He does for the benefit of others, and never for Himself. He has no need of any of those things which are so necessary for us.

---

* This sermon is taken from *The Metropolitan Tabernacle Pulpit* and was intended for reading on Sunday, August 28, 1898. It was preached at New Park Street Chapel, Southwark, on an autumn evening in the year 1856.

† The old word "husbandman" means farmer.

Remember how He spoke to Israel of old: "I will take no bullock out of your house, no he goats out of your folds. For every beast of the forest is mine, and the cattle upon a thousand hills. I know all the fowls of the mountains: and the wild beasts of the field are mine. If I were hungry, I would not tell you: for the world is mine, and the fullness thereof." All things are God's and all He does in creation, all the works of His providence, are not done for Himself, but for His creatures, out of the benevolence of His loving heart.

And in spiritual matters, also, God is a great Husbandman; and there, too, all His works are done for His people, that they may be fed and satisfied, as with marrow and fatness. Permit me, then, to refer you to the great gospel fields which our Heavenly Father farms for the good of His children. There is a great variety of them, but they are all on good soil, for the words of Moses are true of the spiritual Israel: "The fountains of Jacob shall be upon a land of corn and wine; also his heavens shall drop down dew." God, as the great spiritual Husbandman, has many fields, but they are all fertile, and there is always an abundant harvest to be reaped in them.

One field is called *doctrine field*. Oh, what large sheaves of blessed corn are to be found there! He who does but glean in it will find great spiritual nutriment. There is the great sheaf of election, full, indeed, of heavy ears of corn like Pharaoh saw in his first dream, "fat and good." There is the great sheaf of preservation, wherein it is promised to us that the work God has begun He will assuredly complete. And if we have not faith enough to partake of either of these sheaves, there is the most blessed sheaf of all— ay, it is many sheaves in one—the sheaf of redemption by the blood of Christ. Many a poor soul, who could not feed on electing love, has found satisfaction in the blood of Jesus. He could sit down, and rejoice that redemption is finished, and that for ever penitent soul there is provided a great atonement, whereby he is reconciled to God.

I cannot stop to tell you of all the sheaves in the doctrine field. Some say there are only five; I believe the five great doctrines of Calvinism are, in some degree, a summary of the rest; they are distinctive points wherein we differ from those who "have erred from the faith, and pierced themselves through with many sorrows." But there are many more doctrines beside these five; and all are alike precious, and all are alike valuable to the true believer's soul, for he can feed upon them to his heart's content.

I wonder why it is that some of our ministers are so particular about locking the gate of this doctrine field. They do not like God's people to get in. I believe it is because they are afraid Jeshurun would wax fat and kick, if he had too much food; at least, that is what I must be charitable enough to suppose. I fear that many are like the huge corn monopolist; they buy the doctrine of election, but keep it to themselves; they believe it is true, yet they never preach it. They say that all the distinguishing doctrines of grace are true; but they never proclaim them to others. There are Particular Baptists who are as sound in doctrine as any of us; but, unfortunately, they never make any sound about it; and though they are very sound when alone, they are very unsound when they come into their pulpits, for they never preach doctrine there. I say, swing the gate wide open, and come in, all you children of God!

I am sure there is no noxious weed in my Master's field. If the doctrine be a true one, it cannot hurt the child of God; and so, as it is the truth, you may feast upon it till your soul is satisfied, and no harm will come of it. The idea of reserve in preaching—keeping back some doctrines because they are not fit to be preached!—I will repeat what I have said before, it is a piece of most abominable impudence on the part of man, to say that anything which God has revealed is unfit to be preached. If it is unfit to be preached, I am sure the Almighty would never have revealed it to us. No, like the old man described by Solomon, these preachers, who do not proclaim good, sound doctrine, are "afraid of that which is high." It is a mark of their senility that they fear to talk of these great things. God was not afraid to write them, and we, therefore, ought not to be afraid to preach them. The doctrine field is a glorious field, beloved; go often into it, and glean; you may find there more than an ephah of the finest wheat every day.

Then, next, God has a field called *promise field*; on that I need not dwell, for many of you have often been there. But let us just take an ear or two out of one of the sheaves, and show them to you, that you may be tempted to go into the field to glean more for yourselves. Here is one: "The mountains shall depart, and the hills be removed; but my kindness shall not depart from thee, neither shall the covenant of my peace be removed, saith the Lord that hath mercy on thee." There is a heavy ear for you, now for another: "When thou passest through the waters, I will be with thee; and through the rivers, they shall not overflow thee: when thou walkest through the fire, thou shalt not be burned; neither shall the flame kindle upon thee."

Here is another; it has a short stalk, but there is a great deal of corn in it: "My grace is sufficient for thee." Here is another: "Fear thou not, for I am with thee." Here is another one: "Let not your heart be troubled: ye believe in God, believe also in me. In my Father's house are many mansions: if it were not so, I would have told you. I go to prepare a place for you. And if I go and prepare a place for you, I will come again, and receive you unto myself; that where I am, there ye may be also." There is the promise of Christ's glorious second coming; and is not that a heavy ear of wheat for the Lord's children to pick up?

Yes, beloved, we can say of the promise field what cannot be said of any farmer's field in England, namely, that it is so rich a field, it cannot be richer, and has so many ears of corn in it, that you could not put in another one. As the poet sings—

How firm a foundation, ye saints of the Lord,
Is laid for your faith in His excellent Word!
What more can He say than to you He hath said,
You who unto Jesus for refuge have fled?

Go and glean in that field, Christian; it is all your own, every ear of it; pull great handfuls out of the sheaves, if you like, for you are truly welcome to all you can find.

Then there is *ordinance field*; a great deal of corn grows in that field. One part of it reminds us of the ordinance of believers' baptism; and, verily, God's children are greatly profited even by the sight of the baptism of others; it comforts and cheers them, and helps them to renew their own dedication vow to the Lord Most High. But I must not detain you long in this field, though it is to many of us a very hallowed spot. Some of my friends never go into this field at all, it is too damp a soil for them; and though the corn is very fine, and very high, they are afraid to go there. Let us leave that part of the field, and pass on to the place of communion. Oh, it is sweet, divinely sweet, to sit at the table of our Lord, to eat the bread and drink the wine! What rich dainties are there provided for us! Has not Jesus often given us there "the kisses of His mouth," and have we not there tasted His love, and proved it to be "better than wine"? Beloved, go into that ordinance field; walk in the ordinances of the Lord blameless, and do not despise either of them. Keep His commandments, for so will you find a great reward, and so will He fill your souls with marrow and fatness.

But God has one field on a hill, which is as rich as any of the others; and, indeed, you cannot really and truly go into any of the other fields unless you go through this one, for the road to the other fields lies through this one, which is called *the field of fellowship and communion with Christ*. Ah! that is the field to glean in; some of you have only run through it, you have not stopped in it; but he who knows how to abide in it, and to walk about it, never loses anything, but gains much. Beloved, it is only in proportion as we hold fellowship with Christ, and commune with Him, that either ordinances, or doctrines, or promises, can profit us. All those other things are dry and barren unless we have entered into the love of Christ, unless we have realized our union with Him, unless we have a sympathy with His heart, unless we bear His likeness, unless we dwell continually with Him, and feel His love, and are ravished with His delights.

I am sorry to say that few Christians think as much as they ought of this field; it is enough for them to be sound in doctrine, and tolerably correct in practice; they do not think as much as they should about holding fellowship with Christ. I am sure, if they did, there would not be half so many evil tempers as there are; nor half so much pride, and not a tithe so much sloth, if they went into that field more often. Oh, it is a blessed one; there is no such field as that! You may go into it and revel in delights, for it is full of everything good that the heart can wish, or the soul imagine, or the mind conceive. Blessed, blessed field is that! And God leaves the gate of that field wide open for every believer.

Children of God, go into all these fields; do not despise one of them; but go and glean in them all; for there is the richest gleaning in all creation. II. Now, in the second place, we have to think and speak of

A Humble Gleaner

Ruth was a gleaner, and she may serve as an illustration of what every believer should be in the fields of God. He should be a gleaner, and *he may take a whole sheaf home if he likes*; he may be something more than a gleaner if he can be; but I use the figure of a gleaner, because I believe that is the most a Christian ever is. Some may ask, "Why does not the Christian go and reap all the field, and take all the corn home with him?" So he may, if he can; if he likes to take a whole sheaf on his back, and go home with it, he may do so. And if he will bring a great wagon, and carry away all there is in the field, he may have it all; but, generally, our faith is so small that we can only glean, we take away but a little of the blessing which God has prepared so abundantly; and though, sometimes, faith does take and enjoy much, yet, when we compare it with what there is to be enjoyed, a gleaner is the true picture of faith, and more especially of little faith. All it can do is to glean; it cannot cart the wheat home, or carry a sheaf on its shoulders; it can only take it up ear by ear.

Again, I may remark, that *the gleaner, in her business, has to endure much toil and fatigue*. She rises early in the morning, and trudges off to a field; if that be shut, she trudges to another; and if that be closed, or the corn has all been gleaned, she goes to another. All day long, though the sun is shining on her, except when she sits down under a tree, to rest and refresh herself a little, still she goes on stooping, and gathering up her ears of corn; and she returns home till nightfall, for she desires, if the field if good, to pick up all she can in the day, and she would not like to go back unless her arms were full of the rich corn she so much desires to find.

Beloved, so let it be with every believer; let him not be afraid of a little weariness in his Master's service. If the gleaning is good, the spiritual gleaner will not mind fatigue in gathering it. One says, "I walk five miles every Sunday to chapel"; another says, "I walk six or seven miles." Very well, if it is the gospel, it is worth, not only walking six or seven miles, but sixty or seventy, for it will pay you well. The gleaner must look for some toil and trouble; he must not expect that everything will come to him very easily. We must not think that it is always the field next our house that is to be gleaned; it may be a field at the further end of the village. If so, let us go trudging off to it, that we may get our hands and arms full.

But I remark, next, that *the gleaner has to stoop for every ear she gets.* Why is it that proud people do not profit under the Word? Why is it that your grand folk cannot get any good out of many gospel ministers? Why, because they want the ministers to pick up the corn for them! And beside that, many of the ministers hold it so high above their heads, that they can scarcely see it. They say, "Here is something wonderful"; and they admire the cleverness of the man who holds it up.

Now, I like to scatter the corn on the ground as much as ever I can; I do not mean to hold it up so high that you cannot reach it. One reason is that I cannot; I have not the talent to hold it up where you cannot see it; my ability will only allow me just to throw the corn on the ground, so that the people can pick it up; and if it is thrown on the ground, then all can get it. If we preach only to the rich, they can understand, but the poor cannot; but when we preach to the poor, the rich can understand it if they like, and if they do not like it, they can go somewhere else.

I believe that the real gleaner, who gets any spiritual food, will have to stoop to pick it up; and I would gladly stoop to know and understand the gospel. It is worthwhile going anywhere to hear the gospel; but, nowadays, people must have fine steeples to their places of worship, fine gowns for their ministers, and they must preach most eloquently. But that is not the way the Lord ordained; He intended that there should be plain, simple, faithful preaching; and it is by the foolishness of such preaching that He will save them that believe. Beloved friends, remember that gleaners who are to get anything must expect to stoop.

Note, in the next place, that *what a gleaner gathers, she gets ear by ear.* Sometimes, it is true, she gets a handful; but that is the exception, not the rule. In the case of Ruth, handfuls were let fall on purpose for her; but the usual way is to glean ear by ear. The gleaner stoops, and picks up first one ear, and then another, and then another; only one ear at a time. Now, beloved, where there are handfuls to be picked up at once, there is the place to go and glean; but if you cannot get handfuls, go and get ear by ear.

I have heard of certain people, who have been in the habit of hearing a favorite minister in London, saying, when they go to the seaside, "We cannot hear anybody after him; we shall not go to that chapel any more." So they stay at home all day on the Sunday, I suppose forgetting that passage, "not forsaking the assembling of ourselves together, as the manner of some is." They cannot get a handful, and therefore they will not pick up an ear. So the poor creatures are starved, and they are glad enough to get back home again.

They should have gone, if they could get but one ear; and he is a sorry minister who cannot give them *that*; and if they got only one ear, it would be worth having. If it be only six words of God, if we think of them, they will do us good. Let us be content, then, to glean ear by ear; let us take away a whole sheaf with us if we can; but if we cannot do that, let us at least get the good corn an ear at a time.

"Oh!" says a friend, "I cannot get anything from some ministers at all; they preach such a mingle-mangle of truth and error." I know they do; but it will be a strange thing if you cannot get an ear or two of wheat even from them. There is a great deal of straw, you are not required to take that away; but it will be remarkable if you cannot pick up an ear or two of good grain. You say, "The error that the man preaches distresses my mind." No doubt it does; but the best way is to leave the falsehood alone, and pick out the sound truth; and if there is no sound truth in the sermon, a good plan is to read it all backward, and then it will be sure to be sound.

I heard a man of that kind once, and when he said a thing was so-and-so, I said to myself that it was not; and when he said such-and-such a thing would happen, I said it would not; and I enjoyed the sermon then. He said that the people of God, through their sin, would perish, I had only to put a "not" into his sentence, and what a sweet and comforting message it was then! That is the way, when you hear a bad sermon, just to qualify what the preacher says. Then, after all, you can make his discourse suggest spiritual thoughts to you, and do you good. But you must be content, wherever you go to hear the Word, to pick up the corn ear by ear.

Note, next, that *what the gleaner picks up, she keeps in her hand*; she does not pick it up, and then drop it down, as some do in their spiritual gleaning. There is a good thought at the beginning of the sermon; but you are all agape to hear another, and you let the first go. Then, toward the end of the discourse, there is another flash perhaps; and, in trying to catch that, you have forgotten all the rest. So, when the sermon is over, it is nearly all gone; and you are about as wise as a gleaner, who should set out in the morning, and pick up one ear, then drop that, and pick up another; then drop that, and pick up another; she would find, at night, that she had got nothing for all her trouble. It is just the same in hearing a sermon: some people pick up the ears, and drop them again as fast as they pick them up.

But one says, "I have kept nearly the whole of the sermon." I am glad to hear it, my friend; but just allow me to make a remark. Many a man, when he has nearly the whole sermon, loses it on the way home. Much depends on our conduct on our way back from the house of God. I have heard of a Christian man who was seen hurrying home one Sunday with all his might. A friend asked him why he was in such haste. "Oh!" said he, "two or three Sundays ago, our minister gave us a most blessed discourse, and I greatly enjoyed it, but as soon as I was outside the chapel, there were two deacons, and one pulled one way, and the other pulled the other way, till they tore the sermon all to pieces; and though it was a most blessed discourse, I did not remember a word of it when I got home; all the savor and unction had been taken out of it by those deacons; so I thought I would hurry home tonight, and pray over the sermon without speaking to them at all." It is always the best way, beloved, to go straight home from your places of worship; if you begin your chit-chat about this thing and the other, you lose all the savor and unction of the discourse; therefore I would advise you to go home as quickly as you can after service; possibly, you might then get more good than you usually do from the sermon, and from the worship altogether.

Then, again, *the gleaner takes the wheat home, and threshes it*. It is a blessed thing to thresh a sermon when you have heard it. Many persons thrash the preacher; but that is not half so good as *threshing* the sermon. They begin finding this fault an the other with him, and they think that is doing good; but it is not. Take the sermon, beloved, when you have listened to it, lay it down on the floor of meditation, and beat it with the flail of prayer; so you will get the corn out of it. But the sermon is no good unless you thrash it. Why, that is as if a gleaner should stow away her corn in the room, and the mice should find it; in that case, it would be a nuisance to her rather than a benefit. So, some people hear a sermon, and carry it home, and then allow their sins to eat it all up; thus, it becomes an injury to them, rather than a blessing. But he who knows how to flail a sermon well, to put it into the threshing machine, and thresh it well, has learned a good art, from which he shall profit much.

I have heard of an aged Scotchman, who, one Sunday morning, returned from "kirk" rather earlier than usual, and his wife, surprised to see him home so soon, said to him, "Donald, is the sermon all done?" "No," he answered, "it is all *said*, but it is not all *done* by a long way." We ought to take the sermon home, to *do* what the preacher has *said*; that is what I mean by threshing it. But some of you are content if you carry the sermon home; you are willing enough, perhaps, to talk a little about it; but there is no thorough threshing of it by meditation and prayer.

And then, once more, *the good woman, after threshing the corn, no doubt afterward winnowed it*. Ruth did this in the field; but you can scarcely do so with the sermons you hear; some of the winnowing must be done at home. Observe, too, that Ruth did not take the chaff home; she left that behind her in the field. It is an important thing to winnow every sermon that you hear. My dear friends, I would not wish you to be spongy hearers, who suck up everything that is poured into their ears. I would have you all to be winnowers, to separate the precious from the chaff.

With all ministers, there is a certain quantity of chaff mixed with the corn; but I have noticed in some hearers a sad predilection to take all the chaff, and leave the corn behind. One exclaims, when he gets out of the building, or even before, "That was a curious story that the preacher told; won't it make a good anecdote for me at the next party I attend?" Another says, "Mr. Spurgeon used such-and-such an expression." If you hear a man talk in that way, do you know what you should say to him? You should say, "Stop, friend; we all have our faults, and perhaps you have as many as anybody else; cannot you tell us something Mr. Spurgeon said that was *good*?" "Oh, I don't recollect that; that is all gone!" Just so; people are ready to remember what is bad, but they soon forget anything that is good.

Let me advise you to winnow the sermon, to meditate upon it, to pray over it, to separate the chaff from the wheat, and to take care of that which is good. That is the true art of heavenly gleaning; may the Lord teach us it, that we may become "rich to all the intents of bliss," that we may be filled and satisfied with the favor and goodness of the Lord! III. Now, in the last place, here is

A Gracious Permission Given

"Let her glean even among the sheaves, and reproach her not." Ruth had no right to go among the sheaves to glean, but Boaz gave her a right to go there by saying, "Let her do it." For her to be allowed to go among the sheaves, in that part of the field where the wheat was not already carted, was a special favor; but to go among the sheaves, and to have handfuls of corn dropped on purpose for her, was a further proof of the kindness of Boaz.

Shall I tell you the reasons that moved the heart of Boaz to let Ruth go and glean among the sheaves? One reason was, *because he loved her*. He would have her go there, because he had conceived a great affection for her, which he afterward displayed in due time. So the Lord lets His people come and glean among the sheaves, because He loved them. Did you have a rich gleaning among the sheaves, the other Sabbath? Did you carry home your sack, filled like the sacks of Benjamin's brothers, when they went back from Egypt? Did you have an abundance of the good corn of the land? Were you satisfied with favor, and filled with the blessing of the Lord? That was all owing to your Master's goodness; it was because He loved you that He dealt so bountifully with you. Look, I beg you, on all your mercies as proofs of His love; especially, look on all your spiritual blessings as being tokens of His grace. It will make your corn grind all the better, and taste all the sweeter, if you think that it is a proof of love that your sweet seasons, your high enjoyments, your blessed ravishments of spirit, are so many proofs of your Lord's affection to you. Boaz allowed Ruth to go and glean among the sheaves because of His love to her; so, beloved, it is God's free grace that lets us go among His sheaves, or experience blessings. We have no right to be there of ourselves; it is all the Lord's free and sovereign grace that lets us go there.

There was another reason why Boaz let Ruth glean among the sheaves—that was, *because he was related to her*. And that is why the Lord sometimes gives us such sweet mercies, and takes us into His banqueting house, because He is related to us. He is our Brother, our Kinsman, nearly allied to us by ties of blood; ay, more than that, He is the Husband of His church, and He may well let His wife go and glean among the sheaves, for all she gets is not lost to Him; it is only putting it out of one hand into the other, since her interests and His are all one. So He may well say, "Beloved, take all you please; I am none the poorer, for you are mine. You are my partner, you are my chosen one, my bride; so take it, take it all, for it is still in the family, and there is nonetheless when you have taken all that you can."

What more shall I say to you, beloved? Go a-gleaning, spiritually, as much as ever you can. Never lose an opportunity to get a blessing. Glean at the mercy-seat; glean in the house of God; glean in private meditation; glean in reading spiritual books; glean in associating with gracious men and women; glean everywhere—wherever you go; and if you can pick up only an ear a day, you who are so much engaged in business, and so much penned up by cares, if you can only spare five minutes, go a-gleaning a little; and if you cannot carry away a sheaf, get an ear; of if you cannot get an ear, make sure of at least one grain. Take care to glean a little; if you cannot find much, get as much as ever you can.

Just one other remark, and then I will close. O child of God, never be afraid to glean! All there is in all the Lord's fields is yours. Never think that your Master will be angry with you because you carry away so much of the good corn of the kingdom; the only thing He is likely to be offended with you for is because you do not take enough. "There it is," he says; "take it, take it, and eat it; eat abundantly; drink, yea, drink abundantly, O beloved!" If you find a sweet promise, suck all the honey out of the comb. And if you get hold of some blessed sheaf, do not be afraid to carry it away rejoicing. You have a right to it; let not Satan cheat you out of it. Sharpen up the sickle of your faith, and go harvesting; for you may, if you will; and if you can, take a whole sheaf, and carry it away for spiritual food. But if you cannot take a whole sheaf, the Lord teach you how to glean among the sheaves, even as Ruth did in the fields of Boaz; and may He, in the greatness of His grace, let fall a few handfuls on purpose for you for His dear Son's sake! Amen.

9

*Sarah and Her Daughters**

*Look unto Abraham your father, and unto Sarah that bare you
(Isaiah 51:2).*

*Even as Sara obeyed Abraham, calling him lord: whose daughters
ye are, as long as ye do well, and are not afraid with any amazement
(1 Peter 3:6).*

I desire to thank God for having had the privilege of preaching in Exeter
Hall yesterday to a large congregation from the whole of the second
verse of the fifty-first of Isaiah—"Look unto Abraham your father, and
unto Sarah that bare you: for I called him alone, and blessed him, and
increased him" (sermon preached on behalf of the Baptist Missionary
Society on the morning of April 27, 1881). On that occasion I confined my
remarks to Abraham, and tried to make prominent the facts that God called
him while he was a heathen man, one man, and a lone man, and yet He
blessed him, and made him the founder of His people, multiplying his seed
as the stars and as the sand by the sea-shore. I devoutly beseech the Lord
to accept my testimony to His power, and to increase the faith of the many
of His servants to whom I spoke on that occasion. His Holy Spirit gave me
the word; may He cause His saints to feed upon it.

Now, I never like to do an injustice to anybody, and I feel that I did not
in that sermon speak sufficiently about Sarah, though I did not quite forget her. Let us make up for our omissions. If we had Abraham at Exeter
Hall yesterday morning, we will have Sarah at the Tabernacle tonight, and,
maybe, we shall learn a lesson from her holy character as well as from that
of her husband, and the two lessons combined may go to the perfecting of
each other. May our great teacher, the Holy Spirit, now instruct us.

To begin with, let us note *what a happy circumstance it is when a godly,
gracious man has an equally godly and gracious wife.* It is unfortunate

---

* This sermon is taken from *The Metropolitan Tabernacle Pulpit* and was
preached on Thursday evening, April 28, 1881.

when there is a difference, a radical difference, between husband and wife—when one fears God, and the other has no regard for Him. What a pain it is to a Christian woman to be yoked with an unbelieving husband. In a case which I remember the husband lived all his life indifferent to divine things, while the wife was an earnest Christian woman, and saw all her children grow up in the ways of the Lord. The father lived unregenerate, and died without giving any testimony of a change of heart. When our sister speaks of him, it is with fearful anguish; she does not know what to say, but leaves the matter in the hands of God, often sighing, "O that, by a word or a look, I could have been enabled to indulge a hope that my poor husband looked to Jesus at the last."

The same must be the case of a husband who has an ungodly wife. However much God may bless him in all other respects, there seems to be a great miss there, as if a part of the sun were eclipsed—that a part of life which should be all light left in thick darkness. Oh, let those of us who have the happiness of being joined together in the Lord thank and bless God every time we remember each other. Let us pray God that, having such a privilege, so that our prayers are not hindered by irreligious partners, we may never hinder our prayers ourselves. God grant that we may give unto His name great glory because of His choice favor to us in this respect.

Abraham had cause to praise God for Sarah, and Sarah was grateful for Abraham. I have not the slightest doubt that Sarah's character owed its excellence very much to Abraham. I should not wonder, however, if we discover when all things are revealed that Abraham owed as much to Sarah. They probably learned from each other; sometimes the weaker comforted the stronger, and often the stronger sustained the weaker. I should not wonder if a mutual interchange of their several graces tended to make them both rich in the things of God. Perhaps Abraham had not been all that Abraham was if Sarah had not been all that Sarah was. Our first text bids us, "Look to Sarah," and we do look on her, and we thank God if we, like Abraham, are favored with holy spouses, whose amiable tempers and loving characters tend to make us better servants of God.

We notice, next, as we look to Sarah, that *God does not forget the lesser lights.* Abraham shines like a star of the first magnitude, and we do not at first sight observe that other star, with light so bright and pure, shining with milder radiance but with kindred luster, close at his side. The light of Mamre, which is known under the name of Abraham, resolves itself into a double star when we apply the telescope of reflection and observation. To the common eye Abraham is the sole character, and ordinary people overlook his faithful spouse, but God does not overlook. Our God never omits the good who are obscure. You may depend upon it that there is no such difference in the love of God toward different persons as should make Him fix His eye only upon those who are strong, and omit those who are weak. Our eyes spy out the great things, but God's eye is such that nothing is great with Him, and nothing is little. He is infinite, and therefore nothing bears any comparison to Him.

You remember how it is written that He who tells the stars, and calls them by name, also binds up the broken heart, and heals all their wounds. He who treasures the names of His apostles, notes also the women who followed in His train. He who marks the brave confessors and the bold preachers of the gospel also remembers those helpers who labor quietly in the gospel in places of retirement into which the hawk's eye of history seldom pries.

Let, therefore, those here present, who count themselves to be of the tribe of Benjamin, to be little in Israel, never be discouraged on that account—for the Lord is too great to despise the little ones. You are not forgotten of God, O you who are overlooked by men. The Lord's eye is upon the creeping things innumerable in the great sea as well as upon the great. He will observe you. If He sends the deluging showers that make strong the cedars, which are full of sap, and adorn the brow of Lebanon, so He sends to each tiny blade of grass its own drop of dew. God forgets not the less in His care for the greater. Sarah was in life covered with the shield of the Almighty as well as Abraham, her husband: in death she rested in the same tomb; in heaven she has the same joy; in the book of the Lord she has the same record.

Next notice that *it would be well for us to imitate God in this*—in not forgetting the lesser lights. I do not know that great men are often good examples. I am sorry when, because men have been clever and successful, they are held up to imitation, though their motives and morals have been questionable. I would sooner men were stupid and honest than clever and tricky; it is better to act rightly and fail altogether than succeed by falsehood and cunning. I would sooner bid my son imitate an honest man who has no talent, and whose life is unsuccessful, than point him to the cleverest and greatest who ever lived, whose life has become a brilliant success, but whose principles are condemnable.

Do not learn from the great but from the good. Do not be dazzled by success, but follow the safer light of truth and right. But so it is that men mainly observe that only which is written in big letters; but you know the choicest part of God's books are printed in small characters. They who would only know the rudiments may spell out the words in large type which are for babes; but those who want to be fully instructed must sit down and read the small print of God, given us in lives of saints whom most men neglect.

Some of the choicest virtues are not so much seen in the great as in the quiet, obscure life. Many a Christian woman manifests a glory of character that is to be found in no public man. I am sure that many a flower that is "born to blush unseen," and, as we think, to "waste its fragrance on the desert air," is fairer than the beauties which reign in the conservatory, and are the admiration of all. God has ways of producing very choice things on a small scale. As rare pearls and precious stones are never great masses of rock, but always lie within a narrow compass, so often the fairest and richest virtues are to be found in the humblest individuals. A man may be too great to be good, but he cannot be too little to be gracious.

Do not, therefore, always be studying Abraham, the greater character. Does not the text say, "Look unto Abraham, your father, and unto Sarah that bare you"? You have not learned the full lesson of patriarchal life until you have been in the tent with Sarah as well as among the flocks with her husband.

Furthermore, another reflection arises, namely, that *faith reveals itself in various ways*. Faith makes one person this, and another that. In Noah, faith makes him a shipbuilder, and the second of the world's great fathers. In Abraham, faith makes him a pilgrim and a stranger. In Moses, faith makes him plague Egypt, and feed a nation forty years in the wilderness. In David, faith makes him kill a giant, save a kingdom, and ascend a throne. In Samson, faith makes him slay a thousand Philistines; and in Rahab, it makes her save two Israelites. Faith has many ways of working, and it works according to the condition and position of the person in whom it dwells. Sarah does not become Abraham, nor does Abraham become Sarah. In Isaac, faith does not make him the same royal man as Abraham: he is always tame and gentle rather than great and noble; he comes in like a valley between the two great hills of Abraham and Jacob. Isaac is Isaac, and Isaac has such virtue as becomes him whom the Lord loved; and Jacob, too, is Jacob, and not his father; he is active, and energetic, and far-seeing. God does not by His grace lift us out of our place. A man is made gentle, but he is not made a fool. A woman is made brave, but grace never made her masterful and domineering. Grace does not make the child so self-willed that he disobeys his father; it is something else that does that. Grace does not take away from the father his authority to command the child. It leaves us where we were, in a certain sense, as to our position, and the fruit it bears is congruous to that position.

Thus Sarah is beautified with the virtues that adorn a woman, while Abraham is adorned with all the excellences which are becoming in a godly man. According as the virtue is required, so is it produced. If the circumstances require courage, God makes His servant heroic; if the circumstances require great modesty and prudence, modesty and prudence are given. Faith is a wonderful magician's wand; it works marvels, it achieves impossibilities, it grasps the incomprehensible. Faith can be used anywhere—in the highest heaven touching the ear of God, and winning our desire of Him, and in the lowest places of the earth among the poor and fallen, cheering and upraising them. Faith will quench the violence of fire, turn the edge of the sword, snatch the prey from the enemy and turn the alien to flight.

There is nothing which faith cannot do. It is a principle available for all times, to be used on all occasions, suitable to be used by all for all holy ends. Those who have been taught the sacred art of believing God are the truly learned: no degree of the foremost university can equal in value that which comes with much boldness in the faith. We shall see tonight that if Abraham walks before God and is perfect—if he smites the kings that have carried Lot captive, if he does such deeds of prowess as become a man— the selfsame faith makes Sarah walk before God in her perfectness, and she performs the actions which become her womanhood, and she too is written among the worthies of faith who magnified the Lord.

We are led by our second text to look at *the fruit of faith in Sarah*. There were two fruits of faith in Sarah. She did well and she was not afraid with any amazement. We will begin with the first. It is said of her that

She Did Well

The text says, "whose daughters ye are as long as ye do well." She did well as *a wife*. She was all her husband could desire, and when, at the age of 127 years, she at last fell on sleep, it is said that Abraham not only mourned for her, but the old man wept for her most true and genuine tears of sorrow. He wept for the loss of one who had been the life of his house. As a wife she did well. All the duties that were incumbent upon her as the queen of that traveling company were performed admirably, and we find no fault mentioned concerning her in that respect.

She did well as *a hostess*. It was her duty, as her husband was given to hospitality, to be willing to entertain his guests; and the one instance recorded is, no doubt, the representation of her common mode of procedure. Though she was truly a princess, yet she kneaded the dough and prepared the bread for her husband's guests. They came suddenly, but she had no complaint to make. She was, indeed, always ready to lay herself out to perform that which was one of the highest duties of a God-fearing household in those primitive times.

She did well also as *a mother*. We are sure she did, because we find that her son Isaac was so excellent a man; and you may say what you will, but in the hand of God the mother forms the boy's character. Perhaps the father unconsciously influences the girls, but the mother has evidently most influence of the sons. Any of us can bear witness that it is so in our own case. There are exceptions, of course; but, for the most part, the mother is the queen of the son, and he looks up to her with infinite respect if she be at all such as can be respected. Sarah by faith did her work with Isaac well, for from the very first, in his yielding to his father when he was to be offered up as a sacrifice, we see in him evidence of a holy obedience and faith in God which were seldom equaled, and were never surpassed.

Besides that, it is written that God said of Abraham, "I know

Abraham, that he will command his children and his household after him."
There is one trait in Abraham's character that, wherever he went, he set up
an altar unto the Lord. His rule was a tent and an altar. Dear friends, do you
always make these two things go together—a tent and an altar? Where you
dwell is there sure to be family worship there? I am afraid that many families neglect it, and often it is so because husband and wife are not agreed
about it, and I feel sure that there would not have been that invariable set-
ting up of the worship of God by Abraham in his tent unless Sarah had
been as godly as himself.

She did well, also, as *a believer*, and that is no mean point. As a believer when Abraham was called to separate himself from his kindred, Sarah
went with him. She would adopt the separated life too, and the same car-
avan which traveled across the desert with Abraham for its master had
Sarah for its mistress. She continued with him, believing in God with perseverance. Though they had no city to dwell in, she continued the roaming
life with her husband, looking for a "a city which hath foundations, whose
builder and maker is God." She believed God's promise with all her heart,
for though she laughed once, because when the promise neared its real-
ization it overwhelmed her; it was but a slip for the moment, for it is
written by the apostle in the eleventh of Hebrews, "Through faith also
Sarah herself received strength to conceive seed, and was delivered of a
child when she was past age, because she judged him faithful who had
promised." It was not by nature, but by *faith*, that Isaac was born, the child
of another sort of laughter than that of doubt, the child according to the
promise of God. She was a believing woman, then, and she lived a believing life; and so she did well.

She did well to her parents, well to her husband, well to her household,
well to her guests, well before her God. Oh, that all professing Christian
people had a faith that showed itself in doing well!

But never let it be forgotten that, though we preach faith, faith, faith, as the
great means of salvation, yet we never say that you are saved unless there is
a change wrought in you, and good works are produced in you; for "faith
without works is dead, being alone." Faith saves, but it is the faith which causes people to do well; and if there be a faith (and there is such a faith) which
leaves one just what he was, and permits him to indulge in sin, it is the faith
of devils; perhaps not so good as that, for "the devils believe and tremble,"
whereas these hypocrites profess to believe, and yet dare to defy God, and
seem to have no fear of him whatsoever. Sarah had this testimony from the
Lord, that she did well; and her daughters you are, all of you who believe, if
you do well. Be no discredit to your queenly mother. Take care that you honor
your spiritual parentage, and maintain the high prestige of the elect family.

The point that I am to dwell upon just now is this, that she proved her
faith by a second evidence—

She Was "Not Afraid with Any Amazement"

The text says, "whose daughters ye are, as long as ye do well, and are not afraid with any amazement." She was calm and quiet, and was not put in fear by any terror. There were several occasions in which she might have been much disquieted and put about. The first was in the break-up of her house life. You see her husband, Abraham, gets a call to go from Ur of the Chaldees. Well, it is a considerable journey, and they move to Haran. There are some women—unbelieving women—who would not have understood that. Why does he want to go away from the land in which he lives, and from all our kindred, away to Haran? That would have been her question had she not been a partaker in her husband's faith. An unbelieving woman would have said, "A call from God? Nonsense! Fanaticism! I do not believe in it," and when she saw that her husband would go she would have been afraid with great amazement.

When Abraham went to Haran with his father Terah, and Terah died in Haran, and then God called him to go further, they had to cross the Euphrates and get right away into a land which he knew nothing of, and this must have been a sterner trial still. When they packed up their goods on the camels and on the asses, and started with their train of servants and sheep and cattle, she might very naturally have said, if she had been an unbelieving woman, "Where are you going?" "I do not know," says Abraham. "What are you going for? What are you going to get?" "I do not know," says Abraham, "God has bidden me go, but where I am going to, I do not know; and what I am going for I cannot exactly say, save that God has said, 'Get out from your country and kindred, and I will bless you and multiply you, and give you a land wherein you shall dwell.'"

We do not read that Sarah ever asked these questions, or was ever troubled at all about them. The things were put on the camels' backs, and away she journeyed, for God had called her husband to go, and she resolved to go with him. Through floods or flames, it mattered not to her, she felt safe with her husband's God, and calmly journeyed on. She was not afraid with any amazement.

Then, though we do not hear much about her, we know that all those years she had to live in a tent. You know the man is out abroad attending to his business, and he does not know much about the discomforts of home, not even in such homes as ours. But if you were called to give up your houses and go and live in tents, well, the master might not mind it, but the mistress would. It is a very trying life for a housewife. Sarah traveled from day to day, and what with the constant moving of the tent, as the cattle had to be taken to fresh pastures, it must have been a life of terrible discomfort; yet Sarah never complained. Up tomorrow morning; every tent-pin up; and all the canvas rolled away, for you must move to another station. The sun scorches like an oven, but you must ride across the plain; or if the night is cold with frost and heavy dews, still canvas is your only wall and roof. Remember, they were dwelling in tents as pilgrims and strangers, not for one day, or two, nor a few days in a year, but for scores of years at a stretch. It was bravely done by this good woman who was not afraid with any amazement.

Besides, they did not live in a country where they were all alone, or surrounded by friends, for the tribes around them were all of other religions and of other tastes and ways, and they would have slain Abraham and killed the whole company, if it had not been for a sort of fear that fell upon them, by which the Lord seemed to say to them, "Touch not mine anointed, and do my prophets no harm." The patriarch and his wife dwelt in the midst of enemies, and yet they were not afraid; but if she had not been a believing woman she must have often been afraid with great amazement.

And then there was a special time when the old man, Abraham, put on his harness and went to war. He hears that Chedorlaomer has come down with tributary kings and swept away the cities of the plain, and taken captive his nephew, Lot. Abraham says, "I will go and deliver him"; and she might have said, "My husband, you are an old man. Those gray locks should not be touched with the stains of warfare." She said nothing of the sort, but doubtless cheered him on and smiled as he invites some of his neighbors who dwelt near to go with him. She is under no distress that her husband is gone, and all the herdsmen and servants round about the tents all gone, so that she is left alone with her women servants. No; she sits at home as a queen, and fears no robbers, calmly confident in her God. Abraham has gone to battle, and she fears not for him, and she needs not, for he smites the kings, and they are given like driven stubble to his bow, and he comes back victorious. God was pleased with Sarah's quiet faith, because in troublous times she was not afraid with any amazement.

Then there came, a little while after, that great trial of faith which must have touched Sarah, though its full force fell on her husband. She observed the sudden disappearance of her husband and his servant. "Where is your master? He does not come in to breakfast." The servants say, "He was up a great while before day, and he has gone with the servant, and with the ass, and with Isaac." He had not told her; for Abraham had struggled enough with himself to take Isaac away to the mountain and offer him, and he could not bear to repeat the struggle in Sarah. He was gone without telling Sarah of his movements.

This was a new state of things for her. He did not return all day. "Where has your master gone? I never knew him go away before without informing me. And where is Isaac?" Oh, that Isaac! How she feared for her jewel, her delight, the child of promise, the wonder of her old age. He did not come home that night, nor Abraham either; nor the next day, nor the next. Three days passed, and I can hardly picture the anxiety that would have fallen upon any one of you if you had been Sarah, unless you had enjoyed Sarah's faith, for by faith in this trying case she was not afraid with any amazement.

I dare say it took three days for Abraham to come back again, so that it was a week nearly, and no Abraham and no Isaac. One would have thought she would have wandered about, crying, "Where is my husband, and where is my son?" But not so. She calmly waited, and said within herself, "If he has gone, he has gone upon some necessary errand, and he will be under God's protection; and God who promised to bless him and to bless his seed will not allow any evil to harm him. So she rested quietly, when others would have been in dire dismay. She was not afraid with any amazement. We hear so little said about Sarah, that I am obliged thus to picture what I feel she must have been, because human nature is so like itself, and the effect of events upon us is very like the effect which would have been produced upon the mind of Sarah.

Now, this is a point in which Christian women, and, for the matter of that, Christian men also, should seek to imitate Sarah: we should not let our hearts be troubled, but rest in the Lord, and wait patiently for Him.

What is this virtue? It is a calm, quiet trusting in God. It is freedom from fear, such as is described in another place in these words: "He shall not be afraid of evil tidings: his heart is fixed, trusting in the Lord." Or, as we read in David's words the other night, "Yea, though I walk through the valley of the shadow of death, I will fear no evil: for thou art with me; thy rod and thy staff they comfort me." It is composure of mind, freedom from anxiety, the absence of fretfulness, and clean deliverance from alarm; so that, whatever happens, trepidation does not seize upon the spirit, but the heart keeps on at its own quiet pace, delighting itself in a faithful God. This is the virtue which is worth a king's ransom, and Sarah had it. "Whose daughters ye are if ye are not afraid with any amazement."

When is this virtue to be exercised by us? Well, it should be exercised at all times. If we are not self-composed when we are happy we are not likely to be calm when we are sad. I notice that if I am at all pleased with the praise of a friend, I become in that degree open to be grieved by the censure of a foe. By so much as you are elated by prosperity, by so much are you likely to be depressed when the adversity comes; but if you are calm, quiet, happy—no more than that—when everything goes well, then you will be calm, quiet, happy—not less than that—when everything goes poorly. To keep up an equable frame of mind is a thing to aim at, even as the gardener desires an even temperature for his choice flowers.

You inquire, *Who are to exercise this virtue?* We are all to do so; but the text is specially directed to the sisterhood. I suppose women are exhorted to it, because some of them are rather excitable, a little hysterical, and apt to be depressed and utterly carried away. I am not saying that this fault is general or common among women, neither am I blaming them, but only stating the fact that some are thus afflicted, and it is a happy, happy thing if they can master it, so that they are not afraid with any amazement.

But this virtue especially serves in *times of trouble*, when a very serious trial threatens us. Then the Christian is not to say, "What shall I do now? I shall never endure it. I cannot live through it. Surely God has forgotten me. This trouble will crush me. I shall die of a broken heart." No. No. No. Do not talk so. My dear friend, do not talk so. If you are God's child do not even think so. Try in patience to lift up your head, and remember Sarah, "whose daughters ye are if ye are not afraid with any amazement." And so must it be in times of *personal sickness*. How many are the pains and sufferings that fall to the lot of the sisterhood! But if you have faith you will not be afraid with any amazement. I saw one the other day who was about to go under the surgeon's knife. It was a serious operation, about which all stood in doubt; but I was happy to see her as composed in the prospect of it as though it had been a pleasure rather than a pain. Thus calmly resigned should a Christian be.

I went to see yesterday an aged sister—a member of this church, close upon fourscore years of age: she is dying with dropsy (excess fluids in the body), and, being unable to lie down in bed, is obliged to sit up always—a posture which allows little or no rest. When I entered her room she welcomed me most heartily, which, perhaps was not wonderful, for she was greatly attached to her minister; the wonder lay in the fact that she expressed herself as being full of happiness, full of delight, full of expectancy of being with Christ. I went to comfort her; but she comforted me. What could I say? She talked of the goodness of God with an eye as full of pleasure as if she had been a maiden speaking to her young companion of her marriage day.

Our sister used to sit just there, in yonder pew. I seem to see her sitting there now, but she will soon sit among the bright ones in heaven. I was charmed to see one with such evident marks of long-continued pain upon her face, but with such sweet serenity there too—yea, with more than serenity—with unspeakable joy in the Lord, such as I fear some in health and strength have not yet learned. A Christian woman should not be afraid with any amazement either in adversity or in sickness, but her holy patience should prove her to be a true daughter of Sarah and Abraham.

Christian women in Peter's day were subject to *persecution* as much as their husbands. They were shut up in prison, scourged, tortured, burned, or slain with the sword. One holy woman in the early days of the church was tossed upon the horns of bulls; another was made to sit in a red-hot iron chair: thus were they tortured, not accepting deliverance. In the early days of martyrdom the women were as courageous as the men. They defied the tyrant to do his worst upon their mortal bodies, for their conquering spirits laughed at every torment. If persecuting times should come again, or if they are here already in some measure, O daughters of Sarah, do well, and do not be afraid with any amazement.

And so if you should be called to some *stern duty*, if you should be bound to do what you feel you cannot do, recollect that anybody can do what he can do. It is the believing man who does what he cannot do. We achieve impossibilities by the power of the Almighty God. Do not be afraid, then, of any duty, but believe that you will be able to do it, for grace will be sufficient for you.

At last, in the prospect of death, my dear friends, may you not be afraid with any amazement! Oftentimes a deathbed is vantage-ground for a Christian. Where others show their fear, and sometimes their terror, there should the believer show his peacefulness and his happy expectancy, not afraid with any amazement, whatever the form of death may be.

Now, *what is the excellence of this virtue?* I shall answer that question by saying it is *due to God* that we should not be afraid with any amazement. Such a God as we have ought to be trusted. Under the shadow of such a wing fear becomes a sin. If God were other than He is we might be afraid; but while He is such a God it is due to Him that fear be banished. Peacefulness is true worship. Quiet under alarming conditions is devotion. He worships best who is most calm in evil times.

Moreover, the excellence of this virtue is that it is *most impressive to men*. I do not think anything is more likely to impress the ungodly than the quiet peace of mind of a Christian in danger or near to death. If we can be happy then, our friends will ask, "What makes them so calm?" Nor is the usefulness confined to others. It is *most useful to ourselves*; for he who can be calm in time of trouble will be most likely to make his way through it. When you once become afraid you cannot judge wisely as to your best course. You generally do wrong when you are frightened out of your confidence in God. When the heart begins palpitating, then the whole system is out of order for the battle of life. Be calm, and watch your opportunity.

Napoleon's victories were to a large extent due to the serenity of that masterly warrior; and, depend upon it, it is so with you Christian people. You will win if you can wait. Do not be in a hurry. Consider what you should do. Do not be so alarmed as to make haste. Be patient; be quiet; wait God's time, and so wait your own time. Wait upon God to open your mouth. Ask Him to guide your hand, and to do everything for you. Calmness of mind is the mother of prudence and discretion; it gives the firm foothold which is needful for the warrior when he is about to deal a victorious blow. Those who cannot be amazed by fear shall live to be amazed with mercy.

"*How*," asks one, "*can we obtain it?*" That is the question. Recollect, it is an outgrowth of faith, and you will have it in proportion as you have faith. Have faith in God and you will not be afraid with any amazement. Early in my preaching days I had faith in God in times of thunderstorm. When I have walked out to preach, it has happened that I have been wet through with the storm, and yet I have felt no annoyance from the thunder and lightning. On one occasion I turned in by reason of the extreme severity of the rain to a little lone cottage, and I found a woman there with a child who seemed somewhat relieved when she had admitted me, but previously she had been crying bitterly with sheer alarm and terror. "Why," she said, "this is a little round lodge-house, and the lightning comes in at every window. There is no place into which I can get to hide it from my eyes." I explained to her that I liked to see the lightning, for it showed me that an explosion was all over, and since I had lived to see the flash it was clear it could now do me no harm. I told her that to hear the thunder was a splendid thing, it was only God saying, "It is all over."

If you live to see the lightning flash there is nothing to be afraid of; you would have been dead, and never have seen it, if it had been sent to kill you. I tried to console her on religious grounds, and I remember well praying with her and making her happy as a bird. It was my being so calm and quiet and praying with her that cheered her up; and when I went on my way I left her in peace.

Depend upon it, my dear friend, unless our own souls have peace we cannot communicate it to others. In this way we must believe in God about everything. It so happened that about that matter—the thunder and lightning—I did believe in God up to the very last degree, and therefore I could not be alarmed on that score; so if you believe in God upon any other subject, whatever it is, you will have perfect peace with God about it. If you can believe God when you are in a storm at sea, that He holds the water in the hollow of His hand, you will be at peace about the tempest. It is the thing that troubles you that you must believe about; and when faith makes an application of her hand to the particular trial then will peace of mind come to you.

This holy calm comes, also, *from walking with God.* No spot is so serene as the secret place of the tabernacles of the Most High. Commune with God, and you will forget fear. Keep up daily fellowship with Christ in prayer, in praise, in service, in searching the word, in submitting your heart to the work of the eternal Spirit: and as you walk with God, you will find yourself calm. You know how our poet puts it—

> Oh for a closer walk with God,
> A calm and heavenly frame.

These go together.

If you would feed upon certain truths which will produce the calm of mind, recollect, first, that God is full of love, and therefore nothing that God sends can harm His child. Take everything from the Lord as a love-token, even though it be a stroke of His rod, or a cut of His knife. Everything from that dear hand must mean love, for He has said, "I have graven thee upon the palms of my hands." When you accept every afflic- tion as a love-token, then will your fear be ended.

Next, remember the faithfulness of God to His promise, and the fact that there is a promise for your particular position. The Lord is at this moment under promise to you, and that promise is registered in His book. Search it out, and then grasp it, and say, "He must keep it; He cannot break His word." He has said, "In six troubles I will be with you." Have you got to number six? He has said, "I will never leave you, nor forsake you," and how can He run back from His word? If He does not leave you nor forsake you, what can you fear? Whatever is coming—poverty, sickness, shame, slander—if all the devils in hell are loosed, and they are all coming up against us at once, yet, if the Lord be with us, we will smite them and send them back again to the internal deep as quickly as the swine of old ran down a steep place into the sea and were choked in the waters. "Oh," says the devil, "I can overcome you." We say nothing to him but this—"You know your Master; you know your Master. Lie down, sir! You know your Master, and that Master is our covenant Head, our Husband, and our Lord." Neither world, the flesh, nor the devil shall be able to overcome us, since we have the promise of a faithful God to protect us.

Many of you here tonight have gray hair, or bald heads. I have always such a large proportion of aged people in my congregation that I can say to you what I might not say to the young folk. We, dear friends, ought not to be afraid, for trials are no novelties with us; we have smelt powder, and been grimed with the dust of the conflict times out of mind. We ought not to be troubled; we have been to sea before. And has not the Lord helped us? Tell it to His honor! He has been a very present help. He has borne us through such things that to doubt Him would be an impudent slander upon His character.

As for myself—and I suppose the language I now use would come from the lips of many here—my way has been strewn with wonders of divine mercy. Trials have abounded, and I am glad that they have: they have been opportunities for the display of divine grace. Labors have been attempted of which some said, "these are visionary schemes." But God has always been better than our faith. We have never been confounded, and I think we ought by this time to have learned that trusting in God is the most rea- sonable thing that we ever do. There are speculations in business, risks even in the most solid trading; but there is no speculation in believing God, no risk in trusting in Him.

He who hung the world upon nothing, and yet keeps it in its place, can bring His people to have nothing, and yet to possess all things. He who makes yon arch of heaven stand secure without a buttress or a prop—a mighty arch such as no human engineer could ever contrive—He can make us stand without helpers, without friends, without riches, without strength, and stand, too, when all things else except that which God supports shall have come down in the final crash.

"Trust ye in the Lord forever: for in the Lord Jehovah is everlasting strength." I pray for you who are most timid, that from this day you may be true daughters of Sarah, and not be afraid with any amazement. God bless you with this gracious help, and you will praise His name. Amen.

10

*Rahab's Faith**

By faith the harlot Rahab perished not with them that believed not, when she had received the spies with peace (Hebrews 11:31).

In almost every capital of Europe there are varieties of triumphal arches or columns upon which are recorded the valiant deeds of the country's generals, its emperors, or its monarchs. You will find, in one case, the thousand battles of a Napoleon recorded, and in another, you find the victories of a Nelson pictured. It seems, therefore, but right, that faith, which is the mightiest of the mighty, should have a pillar raised to its honor, upon which its valiant deeds should be recorded. The apostle Paul undertook to raise the structure, and he erected a most magnificent pillar in the chapter before us. It recites the victories of faith. It begins with one triumph of faith, and then proceeds to others.

We have in, in one place, faith triumphing over *death*—Enoch entered not the gates of Hades, but reached heaven by another road from that which is usual to men. We have faith, in another place, wrestling with *time*—Noah, warned of God concerning things not seen as yet, wrestled with time, which placed his deluge 120 years away; and yet, in the confidence of faith, he believed against all rational expectation, against all probability, and his faith was more than a match for probability and time too. We have faith triumphing over *infirmity*—when Abraham begot a son in his old age. And then we have faith triumphing over *natural affection*, as we see Abraham climbing to the top of the hill and raising the knife to slay his only and beloved son at the command of God. We see faith, again, entering the lists with the infirmities of *old age* and the pains of the last struggle, as we read—"By faith, Jacob, when he was a dying, blessed both the sons of Joseph, and worshiped, leaning on the top of his staff."

Then we have faith combating the allurements of a wealthy court. "By

---

* This sermon is taken from *The New Park Street Pulpit* and was preached on Sunday morning, March 1, 1857.

faith Moses esteemed the reproach of Christ greater riches than the treasures in Egypt." We see faith dauntless in courage when Moses forsook Egypt, not fearing the wrath of the king, and equally patient in suffering when he endured as seeing Him who is invisible. We have faith dividing seas, and casting down strong walls.

And then, as though the greatest victory should be recorded last, we have faith entering the lists with sin, holding a tournament with iniquity, and coming off more than a conqueror. "Rahab perished not with them that believed not, when she had received the spies with peace." That this woman was no mere hostess, but a real harlot, I have abundantly proved to every candid hearer while reading the chapter. I am persuaded that nothing but a spirit of distaste for free grace would ever have led any commentator to deny her sin.

I do not think this triumph of faith over sin is not the least here recorded, but that if there be any superiority ascribable to any one of faith's exploits, this is, in some sense, the greatest of all. What! faith, did you fight with hideous lust? What! would you struggle with that fiery passion which sends forth flame from human breasts? What! would you touch with your hallowed fingers foul and bestial debauchery? "Yes," says faith, "I did encounter this abomination of iniquity; I delivered this woman from the loathsome chambers of vice, the wily snares of enchantment, and the fearful penalty of transgression; yes, I brought her off saved and rescued, gave her purity of heart, and renewed in her the beauty of holiness; and now her name shall be recorded in the roll of my triumphs as a woman full of sin, yet saved by faith."

I shall have some things to say this morning concerning this notable victory of faith over sin, such as I think will lead you to see that this was indeed a super-eminent triumph of faith. I will make my divisions alliterative, that you may recollect them. This woman's faith was *saving faith, singular faith, stable faith, self-denying faith, sympathizing faith*, and *sanctifying faith*. Let no one run away, when I shall have expounded the first point, and miss the rest, for you cannot apprehend the whole power of her faith unless you remember each of those particulars I am about to mention.

I. In the first place, this woman's faith was

Saving Faith

All the other persons mentioned here were doubtless saved by faith; but I do not find it specially remarked concerning any of them that they perished not through their faith; while it is particularly said of this woman, that she was delivered amid the general destruction of Jericho purely and only through her faith. And, without doubt, her salvation was not merely of a temporal nature, not merely a deliverance of her body from the sword, but redemption of her soul from hell. Oh! what a mighty thing faith is, when it saves the soul from going down to the pit! So mighty is the ever-rushing torrent of sin, that no arm but that which is as strong as Deity can ever stop the sinner from being hurried down to the gulf of dark despair, and when nearing that gulf so impetuous is the torrent of divine wrath, that nothing can snatch the soul from perdition but an atonement which is as Divine as God Himself.

Yet faith is the instrument of accomplishing the whole work. It delivers the sinner from the stream of sin, and so, laying hold upon the omnipotence of the Spirit, it rescues him from that great whirlpool of destruction unto which his soul was being hurried. What a great thing it is to save a soul! You can never know how great it is unless you have stood in the capacity of a savior to other men. Yon heroic man who, yesterday, when the house one burning, climbed the creaking staircase, and almost suffocated by the smoke, entered an upper chamber, snatched a babe from its bed and a woman from the window, bore them both down in his arms, and saved them at the peril of his own life, *he* can tell you what a great thing it is to save a fellow-creature. Yon noble-hearted youth who, yesterday, sprang into the river, at the hazard of himself, and snatched a drowning man from death, he felt when he stood upon the shore, what a great thing it is to save life.

Ah! but you cannot tell what a great thing it is to save a soul. It is only our Lord Jesus Christ who can tell you that, for He is the only one who has ever been the Savior of sinners. And remember, you can only know how great a thing faith is by knowing the infinite value of the salvation of a soul. No, "By faith, the harlot Rahab was delivered." That she was really saved in a gospel sense as well as temporally, seems to me to be proved from her reception of the spies which was an emblem of the entrance of the word into the heart, and her hanging out of the scarlet thread was an evidence of faith, not inaptly picturing faith in the blood of Jesus the Redeemer.

But who can measure the length and breadth of that word—*salvation*? Ah! it was a mighty deed which faith accomplished when he bore her off in safety. Poor sinner! take comfort. The same faith which saved Rahab can save you. Are you literally one of Rahab's sisters in guilt? She was saved, and so may you be, if God shall grant you repentance. Woman! are you loathsome to yourself? Do you stand at this moment in this assembly, and say, "I am ashamed to be here; I know I have no right to stand among people who are chaste and honest"? I bid you still remain, yes, come again and make this your house of prayer. You are no intruder! You are welcome! For you have a sacred right to the courts of mercy. You have a sacred right; for here sinners are invited, and you are such. Believe in Christ, and you, like Rahab, shall not perish with the disobedient, but even you shall be saved.

And now there is some gentleman in the audience who says, "There's a gospel for you; it is a kind of sanctuary for wicked men, unto which the worst of people may run and be saved." Yes, that is the stale objection which Celsus used against Origen in his discussion. "But," said Origen, "it is true, Celsus, that Christ's gospel is a sanctuary for thieves, robbers, murderers, and harlots. But know this, it is not a sanctuary merely, it is an hospital too; for it heals their sins, delivers them from their diseases, and they are not afterward what they were before they received the gospel." I ask no man today to come to Christ, and then continue his sins. If so, I should ask him to do an absurdity. As well might I talk of delivering a Prometheus, while his chains are allowed to remain upon him and bind him to his rock. It cannot be. Christ takes away the vulture from the conscience, but He takes away the chains too, and makes the man wholly free when He does it all. Yet, we repeat it again, the chief of sinners is as welcome to Christ as the best of saints. The fountain filled with blood was opened for sinful ones; the robe of Christ was woven for naked ones; the balm of Calvary was compounded for sick ones; life came into the world to raise the dead. And oh! perishing and guilty souls, may God give you Rahab's faith, and you shall have this salvation, and shall with her stand yonder, where the white-robed, spotless hosts sing unending hallelujahs to God and the Lamb. II. But mark, Rahab's faith was a

Singular Faith

The City of Jericho was about to be attacked. Within its walls there were hosts of people of all classes and characters, and they knew right well that if their city should be sacked and stormed they would all be put to death; but yet strange to say, there was not one of them who repented of sin, or who even asked for mercy, except this woman who had been a harlot. She and she alone was delivered, a solitary one among a multitude. Now, have you ever felt that it is a very hard thing to have a singular (unique, extraordinary) faith? It is the easiest thing in the world to believe as everybody else believes, but the difficulty is to believe a thing alone, when no one else thinks as you think; to be the solitary champion of a righteous cause when the enemy musters his thousands to the battle.

Not, this was the faith of Rahab. She had not one who felt as she did, who could enter into her feelings and realize the value of her faith. She stood alone. Oh! it is a noble thing to be the lonely follower of despised truth. There be some who could tell you a tale of standing up alone. There have been days when the world poured continually a river of infamy and calumny upon them, but they stemmed the torrent, and by continued grace, made strong in weakness, they held their own until the current turned, and they, in their success, were praised and applauded by the very men who sneered before. Then did the world accord them the name of "great." But where did their greatness lay? Why, in this, that they stood as firm in the storm as they stood in the calm—that they were as content to serve God alone as they were to run by fifties.

To be good we must be singular. Christians must swim against the stream. Dead fish always float down the stream, but the living fish forces its way against the current. Now, worldly religious men will go just as everybody else goes. That is nothing. The thing is to stand alone. Like Elijah, when he said, "I only am left, and they seek my life"; to feel in one's self that we believe as firmly as if a thousand witnesses stood up by our side.

O there is no great right in a man, no strong-minded right, unless he dares to be singular. Why, the most of you are as afraid as you ever can be to go out of the fashions, and you spend more money than you ought because you think you must be respectable. You dare not move in opposition to your brethren and sisters in the circle in which you move; and therefore you involve yourselves in difficulties. You are blindfolded by the rich fabric of fashion, and therefore many a wrong thing is tolerated because it is customary. But a strong minded man is one who does not try to be singular, but who dares to be singular, when he knows that to be singular is to be right. Now, Rahab's faith, sinner as she was, had this glory, this crown about its head, that she stood alone, "faithful among the faithless found."

And why should not God grant the same faith to you my poor sinning, but contrite hearer? You live in a back street, in a house which contains none but graceless, irreligious men and women. But if you have grace in your heart you will dare to do right. You belong to an infidel club; if you should make them a speech after your own conscience, they would hiss you; and if you forsook their company, they would persecute you. Go and try them. Dare them. See whether you can do it; for if you are afraid of men, you are taken in a snare which *may prove your grief*, and *is now* your *sin*. Mark you, the chief of sinners can make the most daring saints; the worst men in the devil's army, when they are converted, make the truest soldiers for Jesus. The forlorn hope of Christendom has generally been led by men who have proved the high efficacy of grace to an eminent degree by having been saved from the deepest sins. Go on, and the Lord give you that high and singular faith! III. Furthermore, this woman's faith was a

Stable Faith

It stood firm in the midst of trouble. I have heard of a clergyman who was once waited upon by his churchwarden, after a long time of drought, and was requested to put up a prayer for rain. "Well," said he "my good man, I will offer it, but it's not a bit of use while the wind's in the east, I'm sure." There are many who have that kind of faith: they believe just so far as probabilities go with them, but when the promise and the probability part, then they follow the probability and part the promise. They say, "The thing is likely, therefore I believe it." But that is no faith, it is sight. True faith exclaims, "The thing is unlikely, yet I believe it." This is real faith. Faith is to say, that "Mountains, when in darkness hidden, are as real as in day." Faith is to look through that cloud, not with the eye of sight, which sees nothing, but with the eye of faith, which sees everything, and to say, "I trust him when I cannot trace him; I tread the sea as firmly as I would the rock; I walk as securely in the tempest as in the sunshine, and lay myself to rest upon the surging billows of the ocean as contentedly as upon my bed." The faith of Rahab was the right sort of faith, for it was firm and enduring.

I will just have a little talk with Rahab this morning, as I suppose old Unbelief did commune with her. Now, my good woman, don't you see the absurdity of this thing? Why, the people of Israel are on the other side of Jordan, and there is no bridge: how are they to get over? Of course they must go up higher toward the fords; and then Jericho will be for a long time secure. They will take other cities before coming to Jericho; and beside, the Canaanites are mighty, and the Israelites are only a parcel of slaves; they will soon be cut in pieces and there will be an end of them; therefore do not harbor these spies.

Why put your life in jeopardy for such an improbability? "Ah," says she, "I do not care about the Jordan; my faith can believe across the Jordan, or else it were only a dry-land faith." By-and-by they march through the Jordan dryshod, then faith gets firmer confidence. "Ah," says she, secretly within herself, what she would willingly have said to her neighbors, "Will you not now believe? Will you not now sue for mercy?" "No," they say, "the walls of Jericho are strong: can the feeble host resist us?" And lo, on the morrow the troops are out, and what do they do? They simply blow a number of rams' horns: her neighbors say, "Why, Rahab, you do not mean to say you believe now? They are mad." The people just go around the city, and all hold their tongues except the few priests blowing rams' horns. "Why, it is ridiculous. It were quite a new thing in warfare to hear of men taking a city by blowing rams' horns."

That was the first day; probably the next day Rahab thought they would come with scaling ladders and mount the walls; but no, rams' horns again, up to the seventh day; and this woman kept the scarlet thread in the window all the time, kept her father and mother and brothers and sisters in the house, and would not let them go out; and on the seventh day when the people made a great shout, the wall of the city fell flat to the ground; but her faith overcame her womanly timidity, and she remained within, although the wall was tumbling to the ground. Rahab's house stood alone upon the wall, a solitary fragment amid a universal wreck, and she and her household were all saved.

Now would you have thought that such a rich plant would grow in such poor soil—that strong faith could grow in such a sinful heart as that of Rahab? Ah! but here it is that God exercises His great husbandry. "My

Father is the husbandman," said Christ. Any husbandman (farmer) can get a good crop out of good soil; but God is the husbandman who can grow cedars on rocks, who cannot only put the hyssop upon the wall, but put the oak there too, and make the greatest faith spring up in the most unlikely position. All glory to His grace! The greatest sinner may become great in faith. Be of good cheer, then, sinner! If Christ should make you repent, you have no need to think that you shall be the least in the family. Oh! no, your name may yet be written among the mightiest of the mighty, and you may stand as a memorable and triumphant instance of the power of faith. IV. This woman's faith was a

Self-Denying Faith

She dared to risk her life for the sake of the spies. She knew that if they were found in her house she would be put to death, but though she was so weak as to do a sinful deed to preserve them, yet she was so *strong* that she would run the risk of being put to death to save these two men. It is something to be able to deny yourselves. A man once said, "I have got a good religion; it's the right sort of religion; I do not know that it costs me a cent a year; and yet I believe I am as truly a religious man as anybody." "Ah!" said one who heard it, "the Lord have mercy on your miserable stingy soul; for if you had been saved you would not have been content with a cent a year"—a half-penny per annum! I hazard this assertion, that there is nothing in the faith of that man who does not exercise self-denial. If we never give anything to Christ's cause, work for Christ, deny ourselves for Christ, the root of the matter is not in us. I might call some of you hypocrites: you sing—

> And if I might make some reserve,
> And duty did not call,
> I love my God with zeal so great,
> That I could give Him all.

Yes, *but you would not though*; you know better than that, for you do not, as it is, give all, no, nor yet half, nor yet the thousandth part. I suppose you think you are *poor* yourselves, though you have some thousand pounds odd a year, and so you keep it yourself, under the notion that "He that giveth to the poor lendeth to the Lord." I don't know how else it is you make your religion square with itself, and be at all consistent. This woman said, "If I must die for these men, I will; I am prepared, bad name as I have, to have worse name still; as a traitor to my country I am prepared to be handed down to infamy, if it be necessary, for having betrayed my country in taking in these spies, for I know it is God's will it should be done, and do it I will at every hazard." O men and women, do not trust your faith, unless it has self-denial with it. Faith and self-denial, like the Siamese twins, are born together, and must live together, and the food that nourishes one must nourish both. But this woman, poor sinner as she was, would deny herself. She brought her life, even as that other woman who was a sinner brought the alabaster box of precious ointment, and broke it on the head of Christ. V. Not to detain you too long, another point very briefly. This woman's faith was a

Sympathizing Faith

She did not believe for herself only; she desired mercy for her relations. Said she, "I want to be saved, but that very desire makes me want to have my father saved, and my mother saved, and my brother saved, and my sister saved." I know a man who walks seven miles every Sunday to hear the gospel preached at a certain place—a place where they preach *the* gospel. You know that very particular, superfine sort—*the* gospel, a gospel, the spirit of which consists in bad temper, carnal security, arrogance, and a seared conscience; but this man was one day met by a friend, who said to him, "Where is your wife?" "*Wife?*" said he to him. "What! does she not come with you?" "Oh, no," said the man; "she never goes anywhere." "Well, but," said he, "don't you try to get her to go, and the children?" "No; the fact of it is, I think, if I look to myself, that is quite enough." "Well," said the other, "and you believe you are God's elect, do you?" "Yes." "Well then," said the other, "I don't think you are, because you are worse than a heathen man and a publican, for you don't care for your own household; therefore I don't think you give much evidence of being God's elect, for they love their fellow-creatures."

So sure as your faith is real, it will want to bring others in. You will say, "You want to make proselytes." Yes; and you will reply that Christ said to the Pharisees, "You compass sea and land to make one proselyte." Yes, and Christ did not find fault with them for doing so; what He found fault with them for, was this—"When you have found him you make him tenfold more the child of hell than yourselves."

The spirit of proselyting is the spirit of Christianity, and we ought to be desirous of possessing it. If any man will say, "I believe such-and-such a thing is true, but I do not wish anyone else to believe it, I will tell you it is a lie; he does not believe it, for it is impossible, heartily and really, to believe a thing, without desiring to make others believe the same. And I am sure of this, moreover, it is impossible to know the value of salvation without desiring to see others brought in. That renowned preacher, Whitefield, said, "As soon as I was converted I wanted to be the means of the conversion of all I had ever known. There were a number of young men that I had played cards with, that I had sinned with, and transgressed with; the first thing I did was, I went to their house to see what I could do for their salvation, nor could I rest until I had the pleasure of seeing many of them brought to the Savior."

This is a firstfruit of the Spirit. It is a kind of instinct in a young Christian. He must have other people feel what he feels. Says one young man, in writing to me this week, "I have been praying for my fellow-clerk in the office; I have desired that he might be brought to the Savior, but at present there is no answer to my prayer." Do not give a penny for that man's piety which will not spread itself. Unless we desire others to taste the benefits we have enjoyed, we are either inhuman monsters or outrageous hypocrites; I think the last is most likely. But this woman was so strong in faith that all her family were saved from destruction.

Young woman! you have a father, and he hates the Savior. O pray for him! Mother! you have a son: he scoffs at Christ. Cry out to God for him. Ay, my friends—young people like myself—we little know what we owe to the prayers of our parents. I feel that I shall never be able sufficiently to bless God for a praying mother. I thought it was a great nuisance to be had in at such a time to pray, and more especially to be made to cry, as my mother used to make me cry. I would have laughed at the idea of anyone else talking to me about these things; but when she prayed, and said, "Lord, save my son Charles," and then was overcome, and could not get any further for crying, you could not help crying too; you could not help *feeling*. It was of no use trying to stand against it.

Ah! and there you are, young man! Your mother is dying, and one thing which makes her deathbed bitter is that you scoff God and hate Christ. Oh! it is the last stage of impiety, when a man can think lightly of a mother's feelings. I would hope there are none such here, but that those of you who have been so blessed, as to have been begotten and brought forth by pious men and women, may take this into consideration—that to perish with a mother's prayers is to perish fearfully; for if a mother's prayers do not bring us to Christ, they are like drops of oil dropped into the flames of hell that will make them burn more fiercely upon the soul forever and ever. Take heed of rushing to perdition over your mother's prayers!

There is an old woman weeping—do you know why? I believe she has sons too, and she loves them. I met with a little incident in company the other day after preaching. There was a little boy at the corner of the table, and his father asked him, "Why does your father love you, John?" Said the dear little lad, very succinctly, "Because I am a good boy." "Yes," said the father, "he would not love you if you were not a good boy." I turned to the good father and remarked that I was not quite sure about the truth of the last remark, for I believe he would love him if he were ever so bad. "Well," he said, "I think I should." And said a minister at the table, "I had an instance of that yesterday. I stepped into the house of a woman who had a son imprisoned for life, and she was as full of her son Richard as if he had been prime minister, or had been her most faithful and dutiful son."

Well, young man, will you kick against love like that—love that will bear your kicks, and will not turn around against you, but love you straight on still? But perhaps that woman—I saw her weep just now—had a mother, who has gone long ago, and she was married to a brutal husband, and at last left a poor widow; she calls to mind the days of her childhood, when the big Bible was brought out and read around the hearth, and "Our Father which are in heaven" was their nightly prayer. Now, perhaps, God is beginning some good thing in her heart. Oh! that He would bring her now, though seventy years of age, to love the Savior! Then would she have the beginning of life over again in her last days, which will be made her best days. VI. One more head, and then we have done. Rahab's faith was a

Sanctifying Faith

Did Rahab continue a harlot after she had faith? No, she did not. I do not believe she was a harlot at the time the men went to her house, though the name still stuck to her, as such bad names will; but I am sure she was not afterward, for Salmon the prince of Judah married her, and her name is put down among the ancestors of our Lord Jesus Christ. She became after that a woman eminent for piety, walking in the fear of God. Now, you may have a dead faith which will ruin your soul. The faith that will save you is a faith which sanctifies.

"Ah!" says the drunkard, "I like the gospel, sir; I believe in Christ." Then he will go over to the Blue Lion tonight and get drunk. Sir, that is not the believing in Christ that is of any use. "Yes," says another, "I believe in Christ"; and when he gets outside he will begin to talk lightly, frothy words, perhaps lascivious ones, and sin as before. Sir, you speak falsely; you do not believe in Christ. That faith which saves the soul is a real faith, and a real faith sanctifies men. It makes them say, "Lord, You have forgiven me my sins; I will sin no more. You have been so merciful to me, I will renounce my guilt; so kindly have You treated me, so lovingly have you embraced me, Lord, I will serve You till I die; and if You will give me grace, and help me so to be, I will be as holy as You are."

You cannot have faith, and yet live in sin. To believe is to be holy. The two things must go together. That faith is a dead faith, a corrupt faith, a rotten faith, which lives in sin that grace may abound.

Rahab was a sanctified woman. Oh that God might so sanctify some of you here! The world has been trying all manner of processes to reform men: there is but one thing that ever will reform them, and that is, faith in the preached gospel. But in this age preaching is much despised. You read the newspaper; you read the book; you hear the lecturer; you sit and listen to the pretty essayist; but where is the preacher? Preaching is not taking out a manuscript sermon, asking God to direct your heart, and then reading pages prepared beforehand. That is reading—not preaching.

There is a good tale told of an old man whose minister used to read. The minister called to see him, and said, "What are you doing, John?" "Why, I'm prophesying, sir." "Prophesying; how is that? You mean you are reading the prophecies?" "No, I don't; I'm prophesying; for you read preaching, and call it preaching, and I read prophecies, and on the same rule that is prophesying."

That man was not far from right. We want to have more outspoken downright utterances of truth and appeals to the conscience, and until we get these we shall never see any great and lasting reforms. But by the preaching of God's word, foolishness though it seem to some, harlots are made righteous, drunkards are reformed, thieves are made honest, and the worst of men brought to the Savior.

Again let me affectionately give the invitation to the vilest of men, if so they feel themselves to be.

> Come ye needy, come, and welcome;
>   God's free bounty glorify;
> True belief and true repentance,
>   Every grace that brings us nigh—
> Without money,
> Come to Jesus Christ, and buy.

Your sins will be forgiven, your transgressions cast away, and you shall henceforth go and sin no more, God having renewed you, and He will keep you even to the end. May God give His blessing, for Jesus' sake! Amen.

11

The Widow of Sarepta *

And the word of the Lord came unto him, saying, Arise, get thee to Zarephath, which belongeth to Zidon, and dwell there: behold, I have commanded a widow woman there to sustain thee (1 Kings 17:8–9).

The prophets taught us much by their doings as by their sayings: they were as truly prophesying to the people by the miracles which they wrought, as by the messages which they delivered. There was oftentimes a symbolic meaning in their actions; in fact, they were constantly teaching the people by outward symbols, which, alas! those people were usually of too dull understanding to interpret, but which, nevertheless, were a sign unto them. In the case of Elijah, a prophet of laconic speech, who said but little, but said that with a voice of thunder, I do not doubt that the narratives connected with his life, are meant to be to us a kind of acted prophesying, full of richest meaning. Let us see what we can gather, this morning, from the inexhaustible barrel and unfailing cruse of the widow of Sarepta. I know not how it is that I feel bound in spirit to preach upon this incident this morning; but this widow seems to have followed me for the last two or three days, with all the importunity of the widow in the parable, who would take no denial; and I trust that there may be some here for whom I bear, under sacred constraint, a message from the Lord. Grant it so, blessed Spirit, and we will praise your name! I. Our first observation will be, this morning, that the case of this woman of Sarepta is an instance of

Divine Election

We are not now inventing anything of our own. We have the warrant of the great Apostle and High Priest of our profession for this assertion, for when he went to Nazareth and opened the book and preached, did he not

---

* This sermon is taken from *The Metropolitan Tabernacle Pulpit* and was preached on Sunday morning, June 21, 1868.

himself say, "Many widows were in Israel in the days of Elias, when the heaven was shut up three years and six months, when great famine was throughout all the land; but unto none of them was Elias sent, save unto Sarepta, a city of Sidon, unto a woman that was a widow"? Election passed over all the poor widows of Israel who might have been expected, as belonging to God's covenant people, to be first provided for in the day of need, and it lighted in sovereignty upon a heathen, a woman living in a country which had been accursed of God, and given over aforetime to the sword of the seed of Jacob. Election, I say, passed over all the likeliest ones, and pitched upon her who seemed to be beyond the verge of hope, ordaining in mercy that she, entertaining the prophet, should be saved thereby.

Surely, beloved, we have here an instance of *the sovereignty* of electing love. If grace must go to Sidon for its object, why must it select a widow? She seemed to be the least likely person to answer the design of the decree, namely, the sustenance of the prophet. Were there not princes in Sidon with secret stores of food? Were there not merchants who had passed over the salt sea and knew where grain was to be found? Were there not men of understanding who could by their conversation cheer the prophet's lonely hours? Nay, but though they be great or wise or wealthy, God bids His chariot downward roll away from the lofty towers of nobles to the humble cottage of the poorest in all Sidonia's dominions, and a poor widow woman becomes the object of special grace. Here is an illustrious instance of distinguishing grace, yet not such a striking one as mine, nor such a remarkable case as yours to you. I seem as if I can understand God's having chosen you, but I shall never cease to wonder that He has elected me.

> How many hearts thou mightst have had
>   More innocent than mine!
> How many souls more worthy far
>   Of that pure touch of thine!
>
> Ah, grace! into unlikeliest hearts
>   It is thy boast to come;
> The glory of thy light to find
>   In darkest spots a home.

The choice is in every case made by the supreme will of Jehovah, and is not ordered according to the will of man, nor the will of the flesh, nor blood, nor birth. It is not of him who wills, nor of him who runs, but He who rules all things according to His own good pleasure, gives as He wills, and withholds as He pleases; and who shall say unto Him, "What doest thou?"

At the same time it was a most *just* choice. I have never heard any one complain that this widow of Sarepta was thus preserved in famine. And who could complain? For if the whole people had been all subject to the same pinching want, they all deserved it; and if God's special bounty in a single case turned aside the evil by His own remarkable power, shall not the Lord do as He wills with His own? Is our eye evil because His eye is good? So also in the realm you have, go plead your rights, and God will give them to you. God will treat no man worse than he deserves, but, indeed, infinitely better. "He has not dealt with us after our sins, nor rewarded us according to our iniquities." But what if He chooses to give to some His special and abounding grace? Men may argue if they will, but the only answer God will give them is this, "Nay but, O man, who are you that replies against God? Shall the thing formed say to Him that formed it, Why have you made me thus?" But, beloved, although God condescends not to explain His modes of action, nor to prove His own justice, for who is He that He should stand at our bar, and should speak for Himself, and explain His actions?—yet is He always just.

Who are we, the ephemera of an hour, that we should arraign the Infinite, the eternal One, from whose hand we spring? He will do as He pleases. Yet for all this, His throne is settled in judgment, and His scepter rules according to righteousness and truth; and in the daylight of eternity we shall all of us admiringly discern that sovereignty was never dissociated from justice, and that when God did absolutely as He willed, He always willed to do the thing which was upright and just. The choice was as just as it was sovereign.

But what a *blessed* choice it was for her! She saw her neighbors famishing; all over the land the people felt the bitter pangs of starvation, but in her house there was no need, for bread and oil abounded. This was no luxury, but was similar to bread and butter among us, for the Easterns use the oil as we use butter. There was just plain food enough to support, but not enough to gratify delicate tastes. The prophet had lived upon better fare before, when he had meat twice a day, but now he must do without it altogether. The prophet's Master would not have the prophet be dainty about such things.

This woman had enough; meal and oil were to her right royal dainties, when there was famine through the land. And, beloved in Christ Jesus, how blessed are we who rejoice in our election! What food we have! What bread and what oil! What supplies of richer dainties than earth could possibly yield—redeeming grace and dying love! The flesh of Jesus and His precious blood to be our meat and drink! If election brings us such stores as these, let us forever magnify the merciful sovereignty which ordained us to such grace.

The choice of this woman, while it brought such blessedness to her, *involved service*. She was not elected merely to be saved in the famine, but to feed the prophet. She must be a woman of faith; she must make the little cake first, and afterward she will have the multiplication of the mean and of the oil. So the grace of God does not choose men to sleep and wake up in heaven, nor choose them to live in sin and find themselves absolved at the last; nor choose them to be idle and go about their own worldly business, and yet to win a reward at the last for which they never toiled. Absolutely not! The sovereign electing grace of God chooses us to repentance, to faith, and afterward to holiness of living, to Christian service, to zeal, to devotion.

Many would wish to be chosen for heaven, but have no wish to be chosen for holiness: then why does such a one argue at election? If he does not wish it himself, why need he grudge those who have it? Dog in the manger, what right have you to howl at those who rejoice in what you do not care for yourself? You do not desire holiness, then why complain that it is wrought in others? If anyone here wishes to be chosen to holiness, wishes to be chosen to give up his sin, if that be a sincere wish, it is a sign that he is chosen already, for such a wish as that could not grow up in his soul by nature. God must have implanted it. Let him be thankful that he finds it there.

But, beloved, let us never think about proving our election unless we bring forth fruit unto holiness by the grace of God. If you hope you are chosen like this woman, let me ask you are you feeding the prophet, are you exhibiting daily a faith in the living God? Could you, like her, at the Lord's command, take out the handful of meal and oil, and believe that God would still supply you? Are you living as the just do, by faith, in simple dependence upon Jehovah whom you cannot see, but whose promise stands fast to you? If so, you are sure you are chosen to it, for you have obtained it; you may be clear of your election, for you have made it sure, because you have brought forth the fruits of it; you are elect unto holiness, elect to be conformed to the image of His Son, predestinated to be one of the family of which He is the firstborn and pattern. Inasmuch as you are made like Him, this proves that you are ordained to be made like Him, and you may rest and rejoice therein.

I beseech our friends never to be afraid of that doctrine of election when they hear it spoken of. It is not to be controverted about every day in the week, and insisted upon as though it were the whole gospel, for it is only one truth among many, but it is a very precious one. There are certain preachers who get this doctrine into their theology as the organ grinders get a tune put into their barrels, and they can never grind out anything but election, over, and over, and over again. Such persons bring a most scriptural doctrine into disrepute. At the same time, it is an indisputable truth of Christianity, and one full of the richest comfort to the child of God, one which is intended to kindle in him perpetual flames of adoring gratitude, a truth which lays him low, and makes him feel that there is nothing in him, and then raises him up and bids him, like a seraph, adore before the throne.

Distinguishing grace is a fact; prize the truth and hold it firmly; live upon Jesus Christ; bless Him that you are made a partaker of His eternal love. There always will be some who will pervert and wrest this doctrine, as they do also the other Scriptures, to their own destruction, but I hardly think I need stop to speak to them. Still there are some who say, "If I am to be saved I shall be saved."

Did they ever hear of a certain Ludovic, an Italian philosopher, who had imbibed the idea of predestination to the exclusion of every other truth? He could see nothing but fate, and thought religious activity useless. A physician who attended him during his sickness, a godly man, desiring to convince him of his error, said to him as he stood by his bedside, "I shall not send you any medicine, I shall not attend to you; in fact, I shall not call any more, because if you are to live you will live, and if you are to die you will die; and therefore it is of no use my attending to you."

He went his way, but in the watches of the night, Ludovic, who had been the slave of a notion, turned it over and saw the folly of it; he saw that there were other truths besides predestination, and he acted like a sane man. As God accomplishes the healing of the sick by the use of medicines, He usually accomplishes also the saving of souls by the means of grace; and as I, not knowing whether I am elected to be healed or not, yet go to the physician, so I, not knowing whether I am elect to be saved or not, yet will go to Jesus as He bids me go, and put my trust in Him, and I hope I shall be accepted in Him.

Dear hearer, do not trifle away your soul by thrusting your head into doctrinal difficulties. Do not be a fool any more, but go to Jesus as you are, and put your trust in Him, and you will not find this knotty point a terror to you; it will indeed become like butter in a lordly dish to you; it will be to you savory meat such as Isaac's soul loved; and as you feed upon it you will become like the three holy children in Babylon, both fatter and fairer and more lovely than those who have not received this precious truth. II. A second truth we learn from the text is the doctrine of

The Secret Operations of God upon the Human Heart

This is illustrated here, for we read, "I have commanded," and yet we do find that the Lord had spoken a single word to this woman, certainly not by Elijah, and I do not know that there was any other prophet at that time within reach of her. No command had been given, and yet God said, "I have commanded a widow woman there to sustain thee." She does not appear to have been at all aware that she was to feed a prophet. She went out that morning to gather sticks, not to meet a guest. She was thinking about feeding her son and herself upon the last cake; certainly she had no idea of sustaining a man of God out of that all but empty barrel of meal.

Yet the Lord, who never lies, spoke a solemn truth when He said, "I have commanded a widow woman there." He had so operated upon her mind that He had prepared her to obey the command when it did come by the lip of His servant the prophet. Even thus, and blessed be God for this comforting truth, long before the minister is sent to preach the gospel, God prepares hearts to receive the word; long before the actual living message comes as a matter of instruction to them, there have been secret operations, both of providence and of grace, which have been making ready a people prepared of the Lord, who shall be called in the day of His power.

Beloved, there is a time no doubt when the Spirit of God begins to operate upon the heart of saved ones, but even from infancy the grace of God begins to prepare the heart for salvation, and long before conversion all the moral agencies, all the providential afflictions, and indeed all the events of life, have been working together to prepare that character for translation from the kingdom of darkness into the kingdom of God's dear Son. There are gracious operations long before there are operations of the Spirit of grace. I call them gracious because they are directed by grace; though they be nothing more than moralizing, restraining, or awakening operations.

When I come to preach, this morning, I do not know who may be in the crowd, but I do know that I shall preach to a picked congregation whom God has Himself selected, and that I shall speak to some who want me, and to whom I am sent of God. There will be tinder somewhere for my sparks, and though there will be many to whom the discourse will be nothing worth, yet there will be chosen ones to whom it will be the power of God. Still does the widow woman meet Elijah: she may not know why she comes, she may come with a very low motive, as it were only to gather a few sticks, but the Lord has sent her; no one can give God's message to her but the chosen preacher, and she is the woman who must receive His word. So in all places where my brethren in the ministry are preaching, the Lord not only sends His servants, but sends the persons whom He means them to meet. He equally prepares the preacher and the hearer.

It is to be hoped that many here have been hopefully prepared for the reception of God's gospel; for they are the *children of godly parents.* I would dearly hope that when the gospel comes to them they will receive it, because they have seen the proof of it in their mother's piety, and in their father's holiness. I trust that having known, like Timothy, the Scriptures from their youth, they will be like the thirsty land, which gapes with huge cracks, as if thirsting to drink in the blessed shower, and not as the hard rock which turns an ungrateful surface to the gentle dew of heaven. I trust there are some here, young in years, of whom the Lord has said, "I have commanded a little girl, or a young lad, to receive Jesus today."

Many I know have been prepared for the gospel by having *long attended the ministry.* Ah! though you are not saved yet, I hope that God is getting you ready for that day of effectual grace. How have I knocked at the doors of some of your consciences: surely, the mark of the hammer may be seen there now. You have found it hard to sin, though you have gone on sinning. You have been almost persuaded, though not persuaded after all. Still you are not what you once were; you have been sobered; you have been made to think; you have become uneasy; the sinful pleasures which were sweet to you have been abandoned; you cannot altogether shake off the thoughts of eternity, of judgment, and of the life to come. Ah! well, I hope this preparation will not after all turn out to be a bud that does not knit, an up-springing blade that never comes to the ear; but may divine grace even now lead you to Jesus, for today is the accepted time—today is the day of salvation. May you be as ready for the gospel today as the widow woman was for Elijah when he met her with the Lord's command.

Many are prepared by *providential trials.* I have blessed God a hundred times that He does not leave His preachers to do the work of winning souls alone. When I have gone to see the sick, I have felt that my Lord has been there preaching sermons which have touched flesh and blood, and pierced to the very quick, while my words alone would only have gone in one ear and out the other. He has laid that dear child dead, and the mother cannot forget that her infant has gone to heaven, while she is on another road. There is the husband looking down upon the corpse of the beloved wife, and he cannot laugh at death and eternity now; there is space for a word of admonition now. Ah! when you come fresh from the bed of fever, when you come here after having been detained at home by weeks of illness, and weariness, then is my time with you. God has broken up the clods, plowed up the fallow ground, cut up the thistles, and made room for His good seed, so that it may fall where it shall live and grow.

Be thankful for your troubles if they prepare you for the gospel; and if any of you have come up here this morning, fresh from fiery trials, now that you are like the melted wax, may God put the seal on you, lest if you grow cold any more, you may never be melted again, and never have another opportunity of receiving the stamp of the cross of Jesus, the mark of the genuine faith in a bleeding Savior.

Others are prepared for immediate salvation, because *the Spirit of God* is actually resting upon them, though they do not know it. There are the incipient germs of repentance; there is the embryo of faith; there is everything which goes to make the Christian life; but it has not as yet come to such development as to be known to be such. When the minister's voice, or the word of God in the Bible, shall explain and enforce the truth, the person will perceive it, and discover himself to be in Christ.

The observation may arise in some mind, "Well, if this be the case, that God is preparing for the gospel, could we not dispense with the ministry altogether?" This is unreasonable. This, instead of putting the ministry on one side, will have with every thoughtful mind the opposite effect. How it ought to encourage us to preach if there be some who are ready for it! Well may we distribute the bread of life when there are hungry souls waiting for it. Well content may we be to compel them to come in that the house may be filled, when there are the poor and needy under the hedge and in the highways who feel their need of the sacred banquet. How this ought to cheer the Christian minister!

No one is better pleased to go fishing than he who fully believes that he shall catch abundance of fish: no warriors march more cheerfully to the battle than those who are assured that they must win the victory. The certainty of success inspires a person to be doubly earnest. The preacher feels that he should be in arduous labors yet more abundant, when he perceives that all these labors are backed up by the providence of God, and made effectual to the divinest ends. Send your servant to sow the seed upon a rock, and to plow all day thereon, and see if he does not grow weary with his useless labors; but if you give him a good piece of ground to till, it is comparatively light work, for he foresees a crop upspringing.

Even the worst people have this mind about them. I have heard that our military prisoners, when they were punished by being made to carry large shot from one end of the prison yard to the other, did not feel it to be so much a punishment when they saw the pyramid of shot at one end of the yard growing larger and the other diminishing: at last it was resolved to make them carry the same shot from one end of the yard to the other and back again continually, then the sense that they were working very hard and accomplishing nothing made the punishment far more irksome. So would it be to the Christian minister. Give him the conviction that he is really achieving success—success for which God works in his omnipotence side by side with him—and the man becomes strong as the bullock for the draught, strong as the lion for the fight. He can do all things, for Jesus strengthens him.

There are some things which may indicate a preparedness for the gospel. Listen, you unconverted ones, and put your hands into your heart to see whether you have any of these. Some are evidently ready for the gospel because they are out of love with all the world's joys, and are the *subjects of a constant unrest*. They used to be quite satisfied, but they do not know how it is now, nothing pleases them. They were charmed once with the theater, but the drama now seems dull and insipid. The viol and the bowl, the dance and the merry-making—these were once a heaven below, but by some means, they scarce know why, they have lost all enjoyment for them. They have accumulated a little money—they hoped that this would satisfy them—but now they say of it, "Vanity of vanities, all is vanity." Literary pursuits which once engrossed them, give them now no satisfaction.

Now, you seem to me to be the person for whom the gospel is intended. Jesus cries, "Come unto me, all ye that labor and are heavy laden, and I will give you rest." Let us hope that when the gospel comes to you, this unrest, though it is not a saving thing, will prove to have been a preparation for the saving work.

Others we meet with who have a constant *dread of coming judgment*. They are somewhat superstitious, it may be, but still even their superstition may become the foundation for something better. The fear which haunts men so that they can scarcely sleep at nights, the dread of punishment which overshadow them, may in some way lead to the worst of results, but in others it is overruled to drive them to Jesus, who gives joy and peace in believing. Frequently we have met with persons oppressed with great distress of conscience. It is not the Spirit's work, but merely a natural sense of wrong-doing, yet for all this it is a fine joint in the harness for the arrow to lodge in. They feel that they have done wrong; the recollection of some one sin, or of a series of iniquities, haunts them, and they cannot be at peace; let us hope that now these fluttering doves will fly to the cleft of the rock and find peace in the wounds of Jesus.

It seems to me that God has put a preparation for grace in the minds of those who are of *honest* straightforward disposition. I do not want to say anything which could be thought unorthodox, and I do not mean it so, but I think where our Lord speaks of honest and good ground, He did mean that there was a good quality in the ground before the seed came; not exactly a saving work, but a God-wrought readiness for the seed, and that readiness was *honesty*. You cannot do anything with rogues. God Himself seldom saves the cunning, double-minded, tricky person. I do not expect to meet in heaven a single person who was an habitual shuffler on earth; it seems as if such never were converted.

I have met with double-dealing professors, but I do not believe the grace of God had anything to do with them; and whenever I catch members of this church who are not straightforward, I always thing of them, "I wish I had known this before you had entered the church, for I would not have advised the church to accept a double-minded man, let him be as fine a professor as he pleased."

How often are those called by grace who, wicked as they are, are downright honest fellows! Look at Jack Tar, the sailor swearing big oaths, drinking and fighting when on shore, and thinking nothing of it, but at the same time never found doing a mean thing, but transparent as glass. Now, when Jack hears the gospel, he is the very man to receive it, for God has wrought in him an outspoken honesty which is like a furrow for the heavenly seed to fall upon.

Honest persecutors have often become honest martyrs. Take, for instance, the apostle Paul. What an honest man he was! He never received a conviction but he carried it out at once. He was "exceeding mad" against the servants of God, but as soon as he knew that Jesus was the Christ, what a bold defender of the faith he became! It delights me to see in people around me the operations of creation and providence, like secret commands of God, preparing others for mercy, so that when the open command comes with the Spirit of God, they receive it and are saved.

There are other matters of this sort, but I shall not mention them; I only want to bring out the point that, apart from the Spirit, and before the effectual grace of God, there are workings in providence without, and mental operations within, by which human minds are made ready for the gospel, so that when it comes, it is as readily obeyed as was the command of Elijah to the widow woman, because, by some mysterious working, God had secretly moved her to sustain him. III. In the third place, our text affords us an instance of

Accepted Instrumentality.

Here is a woman selected to sustain the prophet: she is poor, and a widow. Brethren, if our heavenly Father had so willed it, the spread of the gospel need not have required a penny of our money; but He has ordained it from the very beginning, that wherever the gospel comes, it should make an appeal to the liberality of those who profess it, for its support. There are some who say that the minister ought not to be supported, and that it is a very high and honorable thing for him to earn his own living in trade. I have no doubt it is a very honorable thing. I almost envy the preacher who is able, like Paul, to carry on business and to support himself; but I must confess I am very well satisfied to be as honorable as my Master was; and as He never carried on any trade from the time he took to the ministry, but was supported by the free-will offerings of His people, it is, so far as I am concerned, enough for the servant to be as his Master, and the disciple as his Lord.

From the very first, when our Lord began to preach, the people entertained Him, and supported Him, and His rule was, when He sent forth His apostles, not, "Pay your expenses, and mind you do not mention anything about money to the people," but "Into whatsoever house you enter, eat such things as are set before you." They were evidently to live upon the people to whom they preached, for, said He, "The laborer is worthy of his hire." Now, why has our Lord been pleased to put it so, that the carrying on of the gospel should always require money? There is something so distressing about the very sound of the word money, that some superfine Christians feel quite ill when the offering plate comes around; they are so heavenly-minded, that the idea of any allusion to Mammon grieves their blessed spiritual-mindedness.

Why did our Lord put it so that there should ever be any need of speaking about funds? Why did He talk of the widow's mites, and sit over by the treasury? Why not abolish the treasury altogether? Surely He was as spiritual as we are: why did He introduce the topic of money, or render it necessary that it should be introduced? Was it not because the giving of something to God is the truest form of worship, especially when you give till you feel you have given? To sing a hymn, to pray, yes, these are well enough, but what hypocrite will not do these?

What really is there of self-denial in these? If we have sung we can sing again, and it costs us nothing; but He who gives something, He who like the Sareptan widow is willing to give of his little all, has given a real tribute to the Most High. There is no shame about that, and of all the offerings which come up before God, I will venture to say that the money gifts of His people are among the most real, and the gifts of the poor when they have to deny themselves in order to give, are as acceptable to Jesus Christ as the wrestlings of Jacob by Jabbok, or the songs of David when he danced before the ark.

May not our Lord have been pleased to address us in Scripture concerning "the collection," because liberality to the Lord's work sanctifies the toils of earth? During six long days the Lord's people are working among bricks and timber, or in the field at the plow, or standing behind the counter: what a dreary thing were this for an immortal spirit if it could not be sanctified to noblest uses! But the Lord enables you to sanctify the labor of the six days by bidding you consecrate of the earnings of the six days to Him, week by week presenting your offering through Jesus Christ. It links earth with heaven; it links your merchandise and shipping, your exchanges and warehouses with the heavenly Jerusalem, and the streets thereof. Instead of degrading religion by bringing it down to connection with Mammon, the demands upon your generosity elevate you, by enabling you to do something for God, and compel this world's toils to yield a tribute to the Lord of all.

There is another reason for the calls of the gospel upon our purses which is not at all a small one. God intends thereby to conquer in His people covetousness and earth-love. He calls upon them to support the cause of religion, not because religion could not exist without them, but because they could not healthily exist without giving of their means to the Lord. Even Christian men would soon grow covetous if God did not take his tithe; if there were no portion for the Lord's poor, and the Lord's work in the world, it would come to this, the greedy shoveling in of all we have, and the putting of it by for our children and our heirs, the adding of house to house, and field to field, till we were left alone in the world. There would be scarcely the possibility of Christianity in us if God did not require from us as a loving token that we should contribute to His work.

Then there is another reason, it puts such honor upon us to be allowed to give to Christ. I do not know how you feel, but when I am permitted to give anything to Him who opened his five wounds for me, who gave heart and soul, and all that He had for my redemption, I am full of delight. When I receive I fall flat on my face, but when I am permitted to give, a hand is laid upon me to lift me up, and I rise honorably accepted with my gift. You would all feel honored if you were permitted to present a gift to a queen, how much more to give to the King of kings! The cattle on a thousand hills are His; if He were hungry, He would not tell us; if He were thirsty, He would ask no drink from us; but yet in condescending love He comes to us, and His church comes to us, *in forma pauperis*, and begs us to assist to support His work among men; and when we give cheerfully to Jesus, we are honored in the giving.

In the case before us, God commanded a widow woman to sustain Elijah. Now, if there must be money found for the church, why does not our exalted Head send a few rich people who shall give all of it, and let the poor go free? The Lord graciously does send a few richer people, who give by far the larger proportion of all religious contributions; but I have always noticed that our Lord will never send a spiritual church enough rich people to let them be able to do without the poor, because His intention is that the blessing of being allowed to give to Him should come as much to the widow of Sarepta as to Joseph of Arimathea. It is His intention that His rich people should give in proportion, but He never wishes that anything should prevent the very poorest contribution their penny, and receiving the consequent blessing. "I have commanded a widow woman to sustain thee."

It was a good thing for the widow woman to have such a task assigned her. She was to sustain a prophet. It was an honor to her, and it was no loss to her. What the Lord's servant took with one hand He gave back with the other; and very often we have seen that if God lets His servants give to Him by shovelfuls, He will return it to them by wagon loads at the back door; He will never be a debtor to His creatures. Of course, if they give to receive again, they do not give at all, they are only investing for themselves; but when they give with a free, willing heart, they shall receive even in this life, and certainly in the life to come, an abundant recompense. Therefore, let the poorest always cast their mites into the treasury. On the first day of the week, let every man lay by in store, be he rich or be he poor. Let none appear before the Lord empty, but bring Him an offering with joyful heart. IV. Lastly, the text is a specimen of

Unexpected Interpositions

Here is a prophet to be sustained. He cannot be hidden away anywhere in Israel, for the king is hunting after him; he must go into another country. Who will support him? Jezebel belongs to Sidon. If therefore it is once known that Elijah is in Sidon, he will be seized. But a widow woman living just on the border is prepared by God to entertain the prophet. None of us would have thought of such a thing, but so it was; God unexpectedly finds the right woman who does the work in the right way, whose very obscurity and poverty contributed to the security of the prophet. Let us believe in the unexpected interpositions of God. He allows His people to reach an extremity, and then it is His opportunity. You have said, "The last card is played," then God has come in. The ship has gone to pieces, the soldiers are talking of killing the prisoners, the sailors mean to get out into the boat and escape, and yet "some on boards, and some on broken pieces, they all come safe to land." Rest upon God, and remember that He has servants everywhere, that He can help you when you have not a friend left, and can turn your bitterest enemy into your best assistant.

And this confidence, beloved, should dwell in the church of God in all the times of her need. How many, in this matter, sail upon the wrong tack! Years ago it used to be thought that if somebody, when he died, would endow a chapel, what a good thing it would be, because then there would be something certain to keep it up; but there has never been, that I have ever known, a single place in our denomination in which an endowment has not proved a crushing curse. The Lord will not have us contrive to do without Him; He will cast us on Himself.

A Church of England paper charges me with wishing to endow the College. I never had such a thought, I would not accept such a thing. I will spend now, at once, all I can get, for the needs of men are great and pressing. Peter and Paul, whatever they had, would have used it personally and immediately for the spread of the gospel, and then left the next generation to do their own work, with the living God to help them as He has helped us. If we should ever come to a point in any of our enterprises, so as absolutely to need help, if there was not any rich person found to help us, God would command a widow woman to do it. If there remained no friend on earth, He would send an angel to do it; but He never will allow any enterprise that is carried on with a single eye to His glory, and with simple faith in His promise, to know real lack; He may try it, but He will not destroy it.

Lastly, this also is true with regard to men for Christ's church. We ought to expect that God will raise up men to preach the gospel in places where we never thought they could be found. He found a widow woman at Sidon to feed the prophet. I should not wonder if the coming man should be found in Whitechapel, or St. Giles', or a Roman Catholic Seminary, or the shoeblack brigade. Perhaps the mighty evangelist and lover of human progress may even be found in so unlikely a place as among the bishops; it may be possible for Jesus to find apostles among the frequenters of the turf.

When God would have the greatest apostle to preach the gospel, where did He find him? Among the bigots, a Pharisee of the Pharisees? When He would kindle a morning star for England—a man who should translate the Scriptures, and deliver the pure truth, where did He look? Why, He found a priest, one Wickliffe, or Lutterworth. When He would send forth a man who should thunder against the Pope—a man with a brow of brass and a heart of iron, to be a bold defender of the faith, where did He look for him? From a monastery He selected a monk with shaven crown. "Come, hither, Luther," said He, "I have commanded you to preach the gospel," and away he came.

The providence of God may yet make Mr. Disraeli the instrument of dissolving the unholy union of church and state. Grace may, in the same way, select the greatest blasphemer to become the most useful preacher of the age.

I am expecting that my Lord will do such things. Every day I expect to hear that there are converts in high places; that the highest Puseyites have left the church, and denounced the ceremonies which once they doted on; that the Roman Catholic cardinals have begun to learn that salvation is by faith and not by works.

Why not? It is what our Master has done before, and all power is given to Him in heaven and in earth. He called a widow woman to feed His prophet, and He has found His instruments in the most unlikely places, why should He not again? He can choose the mightiest trees, and make them fair as the cedar of Solomon's temple. He can raise up children unto Abraham out of the stones of Jordan's stream; He can take men who were full of devils, even till they were called legion, and make them sit at His feet, and afterward tell of the glory of His power.

Rest then in God, you doubting ones. Think not His church in danger. His cause goes on in spite of foes; it must do so. Pompey said once, "I have only to stamp my foot and all Italy will turn to soldiers." God has but to lift His finger, and all the lands shall be supplied with preachers. Charles I threatened the citizens of London, that if they did not behave themselves a little more loyally, he would take away the court from London; but the Lord Mayor replied, "If His Majesty does not intend to take away the river Thames, we shall do exceedingly well after all." Even so, if Jesus shall abide with us, and His Spirit shall dwell among us, we can lose a thousand helps, and fare none the worse. If we can but have the benediction of the Father, and the smile of the Son, and the dew of the Holy Spirit, we shall still rejoice in the Lord, and in His name set up our banners, for He has said, "I will never leave thee nor forsake thee."

12

The Inexhaustible Barrel (The Widow of Sarepta)*

And the barrel of meal wasted not, neither did the curse of oil fail, according to the word of the Lord, which he spake by Elijah (1 Kings 17:16).

In the midst of wrath God remembers mercy. Divine love is rendered conspicuous when it shines in the midst of judgments. Fair is that lone star which smiles through the rifts of the thunder-clouds; bright is the oasis which blooms in the wilderness of sand; so fair and so bright is love in the midst of wrath. In the present instance, God had sent an all-consuming famine upon the lands of Israel and Sidon. The two peoples had provoked the Most High, the one by renouncing Him, and the other by sending forth their queen, Jezebel, to teach idolatry in the midst of Israel. God therefore determined to withhold both dew and rain from the polluted lands. But while He did this, He took care that His own chosen ones should be secure. If all the brooks are dry, yet shall there be one reserved for Elijah; and if that should fail, God shall still preserve for him a place of sustenance; nay, not only so, for God had not simply one Elijah, but He had a remnant according to the election of grace, who were hidden by fifties in a cave, and though the whole land was subject to famine, yet these fifties in the cave were fed, and fed from Ahab's table, too, by his faithful, God-fearing steward, Obadiah.

Let us from this draw this inference, that come what may God's people are safe. If the world is to be burned with fire, among the ashes there shall not be found the relics of a saint. If the world should again be drowned with water (as it shall not), yet should there be found another ark for God's Noah. Let convulsions shake the solid earth, let all its pillars tremble, let the skies themselves be rent in twain, yet amid the wreck of worlds the

---

* This sermon is taken from *The New Park Street Pulpit* and was preached on Sunday morning, December 18, 1859.

believer shall be as secure as in the calmest hour of rest. If God cannot save His people under heaven, He will save them *in* heaven. If the world becomes too hot to hold them, then heaven shall be the place of their reception and their safety. Be then confident, when you hear of wars, and rumors of wars. Let no agitation distress you. Whatsoever comes upon the earth, beneath the broad wings of Jehovah, you shall be secure. Stay yourself upon His promise; rest in His faithfulness, and bid defiance to the blackest future, for there is nothing in it direful for you.

Though, however, I make these few observations by way of preface, this is not the subject of this morning. I propose to take the case of the poor widow of Sarepta as an illustration of divine love, as it manifests itself to man; and I shall have three things for you to notice. First, *the object of divine love*; secondly, *the singular methods of divine love*; and, then, in the third place, *the undying faithfulness of divine love*—"The barrel of meal did not waste, neither did the cruse of oil fail, according to the word of the Lord." I. In the first place, let me speak upon

The Object of Divine Love

And here we remark at the very beginning, *how sovereign was the choice*. Our Savior Himself teaches us when He says, "I tell you of a truth, many widows were in Israel in the days of Elias, when the heaven was shut up three years and six months, when great famine was throughout all the land; but unto none of them was Elias sent, save unto Sarepta, a city of Sidon, unto a woman that was a widow." Here was divine sovereignty. When God would make choice of a woman it was not one of His own favored race of Israel, but a poor benighted heathen, sprung from a race who of old had been doomed to be utterly cut off.

Here was electing love in one of its sovereign manifestations. Some are always quarreling with God because He will not submit His will to their dictation. If there could be a God who was not absolute, men would think themselves gods, and hence sovereignty is hated because it humbles the creature, and makes him bow before a Lord, a King, a Master, who will do as He pleases. If God would choose kings and princes, then would men admire His choice. If He would make His chariots stay at the door of nobles, if He would step from His throne and give His mercy only to the great, the wise, and the learned, then might there be heard the shout of praise to a God who thus honored the fine doings of man. But because He chooses to take the base things of this world, the things that are despised, and the things that are not; because He takes these things to bring to nought the things that are, therefore is God hated of men. Yet, know that God has set apart him who is godly for Himself. He has chosen to Himself a people whom He will bring to Himself at last, who are His peculiar treasure, the favorites of His choice. But these people are by nature the most unlikely ones upon the face of the whole world. People today sunken in sin, immersed in folly, brutalized, without knowledge, without wit, these are the very ones whom God ordains to save. To them He sends the word in its effectual might, and these are plucked like brands from the burning. None can guess the reasons of divine election. This great act is as mysterious as it is gracious. Throughout Scripture we are continually startled with resplendent instances of unlimited sovereignty, and the case of this widow is one among the many. Electing love passes by the thousands of widows who dwelt in God's own land, and it journeys beyond the borders of Canaan, to cherish and preserve a heathen woman of Sarepta.

Some people hate the doctrine of divine sovereignty; but those who are called by grace love it, for they feel, if it had not been for sovereignty they never would have been saved. Ah, if we are not His people, what was there in any of us to merit the esteem of God? How is it that some of us are converted, while our companions in sin are left to persevere in their godless career? How is it that some of us who were once drunkards, swearers, and the like, are now sitting here to praise the God of Israel this day? Was there anything good in us that moved the heart of God to save us? God forbid that we should indulge the blasphemous thought. There was nothing in us that made us better than others, or more deserving. Sometimes we are apt to think that it was the reverse. There was much in us that might have caused God to pass us by if He had looked to us. And yet, there we are, praising His name. Tell me, you who deny divine sovereignty, how is it that the publicans and harlots enter into the kingdom of heaven, while the self-righteous Pharisee is shut out? How is it that from the scum of this city, God picks up some of His brightest jewels, while among the learned and philosophic, there are very few who bow the knee to the God of Israel? Tell me, how is it that in heaven there are more servants than masters, more poor than rich, more foolish than learned? What shall we say of this? "I thank thee, O Father, Lord of heaven and earth, because thou hast hid these things from the wise and prudent, and hast revealed them unto babes. Even so, Father: for so it seemed good in thy sight."

But if there be sovereignty in the choice, I cannot omit another thought akin to it. *What undeservingness there was in the person!* She was no Hannah. I do not read that she had smitten the Lord's enemies, like Jael, or had forsaken the gods of her country, like Ruth. She was no more notable than any other heathen. Her idolatry was as vile as theirs, and her mind as foolish and vain as that of the rest of her countrymen. Ah, and in the objects too, of God's love, there is nothing whatever that can move Him to select them. Hark! how the blood-bought ones all sing before the throne. They cast their crowns at the feet of God, and unitedly say, "Not unto us, not unto us, but unto thy name be all the glory forever."

There is no divided note in heaven upon this matter. Not one spirit in glory will dare to say that he deserved to come there. They were strangers once, and they were sought by grace. They were dirty, and they were washed in blood. Their hearts were hard, and they were softened by the Spirit. They were dead, and they were quickened by divine life. And all the reasons for this gracious work in and upon them are to be found in the breast of God, and not at all in them.

Simple as this truth seems, and lying as it does at the very foundation of the gospel system, yet how often is it forgotten! Ah! some of you are saying, "I would come to Christ if I had a better character. I think that God would love me if there were some good works, and some redeeming traits in my character." Nay, but hear me, my friends, God loves not for anything in us. The saved ones are not saved on account of anything they did; but simply because He will have mercy on whom He will have mercy, and He will have compassion on whom He will have compassion. You are in as good a place as any other unregenerate sinner on the face of the earth; why should not God have mercy upon you? Your merits or your demerits have nought to do with the matter. If God intends to bless, He looks not to what you are. He finds His motive in the depth of His own loving will, and not in you. Oh! can you believe it, that dirty, and filthy, and diseased, and leprous though you be, the love of God can shed itself abroad in your heart? O my trembling hearer! do not despair, for He is able to save unto the very uttermost.

In continuing to regard this woman, I want you to notice that her condition was miserable too, in the very last degree. She had not only to suffer the famine which had fallen upon all her neighbors, but her husband was taken from her. He would have shared with her the last morsel that his weary limbs could earn; he would have bidden her lean her head upon his strong and faithful breast, and would have said, "My wife, if there be bread to be had thy mouth shall taste it; if there be water to drink you shall not thirst." But alas! he was taken from her, and she was a widow. Besides this, he had left her no inheritance. She had no patrimony, no servant. You learn this from the fact that she had not even firewood. Now, there was no reason why she should not have had that even in time of famine of bread, for there was no famine of wood, unless she had been extremely poor.

Such was her extremity that she goes outside the city upon the common lands to pick up a few sticks with which she may cook her meal. She had, you see then, nothing wherewithal to buy bread, for even the fuel she must gather for herself. I told you that her husband had left her nothing, yes, he had left her something; but that something, though much beloved, was but another fountain of trouble to her. He had left her a son, her only son, and this son has now to share her starvation. I believe he was too weak to accompany his mother upon this occasion. They had been so long without food that he could not rise from the bed, or else, good soul, she would have brought him with her, and he could have helped to gather a few sticks. But she had laid him upon the bed, fearing that he might die before she reached her home, knowing that he could not accompany her because his limbs were too feeble to carry the little weight of his own poor emaciated body. And now she has come forth with a double trouble, to gather a handful of sticks to dress her last meal, that she may eat it and die.

Ah, my dear friends, this is just where sovereign grace finds us all—in the depth of poverty and misery. I do not mean, of course, temporal poverty, but I mean spiritual distress. So long as we have a full barrel of our own merits, God will have nothing to do with us. So long as the cruse of oil is full to overflowing, we shall never taste the mercy of God. For God will not fill us until we are emptied of self.

Ah, what misery does conviction of sin cause in the breast of the sinner. I have known some so wretched, that all the torments of the inquisition could not equal their agony. If tyrants could invent the knife, the hot irons, the spear, splinters put beneath the nails, and the like, yet could not they equal the torment which some men have felt when under conviction of sin. They have been ready to make an end of themselves. They have dreamed of hell by night, and when they have awakened in the morning it was to feel what they have dreamed. But then it has been in this very times when all their hope was gone, and their misery was come to its utmost extremity, that God looked down in love and mercy on them.

Have I such a hearer in this audience this morning? Have I not one who is smitten in his heart, whose life is blasted, who walks about in the weariness of his spirit, crying, "Oh, that I were gone out of this world, that I might be rid of sin; for oh, my burden presses upon me as though it would sink me to the lowest hell. My sin is like a millstone around my neck and I cannot get rid of it." My hearer, I am glad to hear you speak thus; I rejoice in your unhappiness; and that not because I love to see you miserable, but because your sorrow is a step to everlasting blessedness. I am glad that you are poor, for there is one who will make you rich. I am glad that your barrel of meal is wasted, for now shall a miracle of mercy be wrought for you, and you shall eat the bread of heaven to the full. I am glad that cruse of oil is gone, for now rivers of love and mercy shall be bestowed on you. Only believe it.

In God's name I assure you, if you are brought to extremity God will now appear for you. Look up, sinner—look away from yourself—look up to God who sits upon the throne, a God of love. But if that be too high, look up sinner to yon cross. He who hangs there died for such as you. Those veins were opened for sinners utterly ruined and undone. That agony He suffered was for those who feel an agony of heart like yours. His griefs He meant for the grievers; His mourning made atonement for the mourners. Can you now believe the word which is written?—"This is a faithful saying and worthy of all acceptation, that Christ Jesus came into the world to save sinners." Do you dare trust yourself now upon the merits of Christ? Can you say, "Sink or swim, my hope is in the cross"? Oh, sinner, if God but help you to do this, you are happy! Your poverty shall be removed, and like the widow of Sarepta, you shall know no lack until the day when God shall take you up to heaven, where you shall be satisfied throughout eternity.

I do not know whether I have made what I intended to state sufficiently clear; but what I wanted to bring out is this: Just as God sent His prophet Elijah out of pure sovereignty to a woman who deserved nothing at His hands, and just as He sent a prophet to her in the time of her greatest misery and sorrow, so is the word of God sent to you, my hearer, this morning, if you are in a similar condition. II. Now, I come to the second point:

The Grace of God in Its Dealings

I would have you notice first of all that the love of God toward this woman in its dealings was of the most singular character. You will notice that the first word she heard from the God of Israel was one which rather robbed her than made her rich. It was this: "Fetch me, I pray thee, a little water in a vessel, that I may drink." It was taking something from that already much-diminished store. And then on the heels of that there came another: "Bring me, I pray thee, a morsel of bread in thine hand." This was rather demanding than bestowing. And yet singular it is, this is just the way sovereign mercy deals with men. It is an apparent demand rather than an open gift. For what does God say to us when first He speaks? He says this: "Repent and be converted every one of you, in the name of the Lord Jesus." "Believe on the Lord Jesus Christ and thou shalt be saved." But says the soul, "I cannot repent, it is beyond my power; I cannot believe—I would that I could believe—but this is beyond my reach. And has God asked me to exert a strength which I have not? Does He demand that of me which I cannot give? I thought that He gave; I did not know that He asked of me."

Ay, but soul, notice what this woman did in obedience to the command. She went and fetched water, and she brought the morsel of bread; and the water was not diminished by what she gave, and the bread itself was increased in the spending of it. When God says to the sinner, "Believe," if that sinner believes, it is not by his own power, but by grace which goes with the command. But the sinner does not know that at first. He thinks that *he* believes: he thinks that *he* repents. Why, I do not believe that the meal which the woman brought to the prophet was any meal of hers: it was meal taken out of her store, and yet not taken out of it; it was meal given her by miracle—the first installment of miraculous provision. And so if you believe, you will say, "I have believed." Yes, it was taken out of your barrel, but still it was not your believing, it was an act of faith wrought in you.

Here is a poor man with a withered arm: he wants to have that restored. Now, you will imagine that the first thing Christ will say to him will be, "Man, I will make your withered arm alive; I will once more nerve it so that you shall have power to lift it." No, He does not say any such thing. But before He gives the man the power He says to him, "Stretch out your hand!" Suppose he had cried out, "Sir, I cannot." His withered arm would have hung dangling at his side till he died. But instead of that the command came; the man had the will to obey, and suddenly he had the power, for he stretched out his withered hand. What! you say, did he stretch out that hand of his own might? No, and yet he was commanded to do it. And so if you are willing to believe, if now your hearts say, "I would believe, I would repent," the power shall come with the will, and the withered hand shall be stretched out.

I do preach continually the exhortation and the command. I am not ashamed to say with the prophet Ezekiel, "Ye dry bones live! ye dead souls live." If this is esteemed the unsound doctrine, I shall be yet more heretical. "Man cannot do it; why tell him to do it?" Why simply as an exercise of faith. If I tell a person to do what he can do, anybody can tell him that; but God's servant tells him to do what he cannot do, and the man does it; for God honors the command of His servant, and gives the strength with the command. To sinners dead in sin the cry is given this morning: "Do you want salvation? Believe on Christ. Would you have your sins forgiven? Look to Him." Oh! do not answer, "I cannot believe, I cannot look." Instead, may the Spirit of God incline your mind, so that you may say, "I will believe," and then you will believe. O may you say, "I will repent," and then you will repent. And though it be not your own strength, it will be a strength given so instantly upon the moment, that you for a time will not know whether it is your strength or God's strength, until you get further advanced in the divine life, and then you will discover that all the strength from first to last is of God. I say that the dealings of divine grace with this woman are to be looked upon as extremely singular in that light. And yet they are but the type and the model of the dealings of God with all whom He saves.

Now, the next point. The dealings of love with this poor woman were not only singular, but exceedingly *trying*. The first thing she hears is a trial: Give away some of that water which you and your son so much require! Give away a portion of that last little cake which you intended to eat and die! No, all through the piece it was a matter of trial, for there never was more in the barrel than there was at the first. There was a handful at night, and a handful the next morning; but there never were two handfuls there at a time. To the very last there was only a little glazing of oil in the cruse. Whenever she looked at it, there was only a little glazing of oil to spread upon the meal cakes. The cruse was never full; there was not a drop more in it than there was at first. So that this woman, the first time she had eaten the meal out of the barrel, might have thought to herself, "Well, I have breakfasted in a most extraordinary manner, but where shall I find food at noon?" But when she went there was just one handful more. She took that out and prepared it, and unbelief would have whispered, "But there will be none at eventide." But, however, when night came there was just enough for the hour. The barrel never filled, and yet it never emptied. The store was little, but it was always sufficient for the day.

Now, if God saves us, it will be a trying matter. All the way to heaven, we shall only get there by the skin of our teeth. We shall not go to heaven sailing along with sails swelling to the breeze, like sea birds with their fair white wings, but we shall proceed full often with sails rent to ribbons, with masts creaking, and the ship's pumps at work both by night and day. We shall reach the city at the shutting of the gate, but not an hour before. O believer, the Lord will bring you safe to the end of your pilgrimage; but mark, you will never have one particle of strength to waste in wantonness upon the road. There will be enough to get you up the hill Difficulty, but only enough then by climbing on your hands and knees. You will have strength enough to fight Apollyon, but when the battle is over your arm will have no strength remaining. Your trials will be so many, that if you had only one trail more, it would be like the last ounce that breaks the camel's back. But, nevertheless, though God's love should thus try you all the journey through, your faith will bear the trying, for while God dashes you down to the earth with one hand in providence, He will lift you up with the other in grace. You will have consolation and affliction weighed out in equal degree, ounce for ounce, and grain for grain. You will be like the Israelite in the wilderness—if you gather much manna, you will have nothing over; while blessed be God, if you gather little you shall have no lack. You shall have daily grace for daily trials.

From this interesting topic, I turn to another that is not less so. Although the Lord's dealings with this woman of Sarepta were very trying, yet they were very wise. You ask me—Why did not God give her a granary full of meal at once, and a vat full of oil instantly? I will tell you. It was not merely because of God's intent to try her, but there was wisdom here. Suppose He had given her a granary full of meal, how much of it would have been left for the next day? I question whether any would have remained. For in days of famine people are sharp of scent, and it would soon have been noised about the city, "The old widow woman who lives in such-and-such a street, has a great store of food." Why, they would have caused a riot, and robbed the house, and perhaps, have killed the woman and her son. Her treasure would have been stolen, and in twenty-four hours the barrel of meal would have been as empty as it was at first, and the cruse of oil would have been spilled upon the ground.

What has that to do with us? Just this: if the Lord should give us more grace than we want for the day, we should have all the devils in hell trying to rob us. We have enough to do, as it is, to fight with Satan. But what an uproar there would be! We should have tens of thousands of enemies pouncing upon our stock of grace, and we should have to defend our stock against all these assailants. Now, I think while it is good for us to have a little ready money on hand, to let our real, sterling property remain in the hands of our great Banker above. Should thieves break in, as they often do, and steal my evidences and take away my comforts—they only take a few loose coppers, that I have in the house for convenience. They cannot steal my real treasure, for it is secured in a golden casket, the key of which swings at the girdle of the Lord Jesus Christ. Better for you to have an inheritance preserved in heaven for you, than to have it given to you to take care of for yourself; for you would soon lose it and become as poor as ever.

Besides, there was another reason why this woman did not have her meal given to her all at once. Anyone knows that meal will not keep in great quantities. It soon breeds a peculiar kind of worm, and after a little while it grows musty, and no person would think of eating it. Now, grace is just of the same character. If you have a stock of grace, it breeds a worm called pride. Perhaps you may have seen that worm. It is a very prolific one. I find whenever I have a little extra stock of gifts, or grace, that this worm is sure to breed in the meal, and then soon it begins to smell musty, and is only fit for the dunghill. If we have more grace than we want, it would be like the manna of old, which when it was laid up, bred worms and stank. Besides, how much better it would be, even if it would keep, to have fresh every day. Oh, to have the bread of heaven hot from heaven's oven every day! To have the water out of the rock, not as sailors have it in the casks for a long sea voyage, where the sweetest water ferments, and passes through many stages of decay; but, oh, to have it every hour trickling through the divine rock! To have it fresh from the divine fountain every moment, this is to have a happy life indeed!

This woman need never regret having nothing but a handful on hand, for she had thus the greater inducement to be frequent in her pleadings with God. After she had taken out a handful of meal, I think I see her lifting up her streaming eyes and saying, "Great God, it is now two years since for the first time I put the hand of faith into this barrel, and now every morning, and every noon, and every night, I have done the same, and I have never lacked. Glory be unto the God of Israel!" I think I see her praying as she went: "Oh, Lord, do not shut up Your compassion. You have dealt well with Your poor servant, and fed her this many a year. Grant that the barrel may not fail me now, for I have no stock in hand; grant that there may be a handful still to spare—always enough, always all that my necessities can require." Do you not see that she was thus brought into constant contact with God? She had more reasons for prayer, and more reasons for gratitude, than if she had received the blessing at once. This is one reason why God does not give you grace to spare. He will have you come to Him every day, even every hour. Are you not glad of the plea? You can say each time you come, "Lord, here's a needy beggar at the door, it is not an idle man who is giving a runaway knock at the door of prayer, but, Lord, I am a needy soul: I want a blessing, and I come."

I repeat it, the daily journey to the well of mercy is good for us. The hand of faith is blessed by the exercise of knocking at the gate. "Give us this day our daily bread" is a right good prayer; O for grace to use it daily with our Father who is in heaven!

Now, what is the drift of all this? Just this: among the thousands of letters that I continually receive from my congregation, I meet with this very common question: "Oh, sir, I feel such little faith, such little life, such little grace in my heart, that I am inclined to think I shall never hold out to the end; and sometimes I am afraid I am not a child of God at all." Now, my dear friend, if you want an explanation of this it is to be found in the text. You shall have just enough faith to carry you through your trials, but you shall have no faith to spare. You shall have just enough grace in your heart to keep you living day after day in the fear of God, but you shall have none to sacrifice to your boasting and yield to your own pride. I am glad to hear you say that you feel your spiritual poverty; for when we know ourselves to be poor, then we are rich, but when we think that we are rich and increased in goods, then we are naked, and poor, and miserable, and are in a sad plight indeed. Oh, I want you to remember for your comfort, that though you have never two handfuls of meal in the barrel at a time, yet there will never be less than one handful; that though you will never have a double quantity of oil at one time, yet thee will always be the requisite quantity. There will be nothing over, but there shall be none lacking.

So take this for your comfort, as your days so shall your strength be; as your needs so shall your grace be; as the demands of your necessity, such shall be the supply of God's mercy. The cup shall be full if it does not flow over, and the stream shall always run, even though it is not always brimming the banks. III. I conclude by bringing you to the point upon which I shall dwell but briefly—for I pray that your life may be a far fuller sermon on this text than I can hope to preach—

The Faithfulness of Divine Love

"The barrel of meal wasted not, neither did the cruse of oil fail, according to the word of the Lord, which he spake by Elijah." You will observe that this woman had daily necessities. She had three mouths to feed; she had herself, her son, and the prophet Elijah. But though the need was threefold, yet the supply of meal wasted not. Boys have large appetites, and no doubt her son very speedily devoured that first little cake. As for Elijah himself, he had walked no less a distance than 100 miles, all weary with his journey, you may consider that he had a considerable appetite also;

while she herself, having been long subjected to starvation, would doubtless feed to the full. But though their necessities were very great at the first, yet the barrel of meal wasted not. Each day she made calls upon it, but yet each day it remained the same.

Now beloved, you have daily necessities. Because they come so frequently—because your trials are so many, your troubles so innumerable, you are apt to conceive that the barrel of meal will one day be empty, and the cruse of oil will fail you. But rest assured that according to the Word of God this shall not be the case. Each day, though it bring its trouble, shall bring its help; though it bring its temptation, it shall bring its help; though it bring its need, it shall bring its supply; and though day come after day, if you should live to outnumber the years of Methuselah, and though troubles come after troubles till your tribulations are like the waves of the sea, yet shall God's grace and mercy last through all your necessities, and you shall never know a lack.

For three long years the heavens never saw a cloud, and the stars never wept the holy tears of dew upon the wicked earth; for three long years the women fainted in the streets, and devoured their own offspring for lack of bread; for three long years the mourners went about the streets, wan, and weary, like skeletons following corpses to the tomb; but this woman never was hungry, never knew a lack; always supplied, always joyful in abundance. So shall it be with you. You shall see the sinner die, for he trusts his native strength; you shall see the proud Pharisee totter, for he builds his hope upon the sand; you shall see even your own schemes blasted and withered, but you yourself shall find that your place of defense shall be the munition of rocks; your bread shall be given you, and your water shall be sure. The staff on which you lean shall never break; the arm on which you repose shall never be palsied; the eye that looks on you shall never wax dim; the heart that owes you shall never grow weary; and the hand that supplies you shall never be weak.

Do you not remember a time in your experience, not long ago, when you came to your wits' end? You said, "I shall surely fall by the hands of the enemy." Have you fallen? Are you not still preserved? Look back I pray you. It is not many months ago since business was running so dead against you, that you said, "I must give it up; ever since I have known the Lord I have had more trials than ever I had before." Have you given it up? You have gone through fires; let me ask you, have you been burnt? Has there been a hair of your head singed? You have walked through waters—and deep waters have they been—have you been drowned? You said you should be, but have you? Have the waters overflowed you? When all God's waves and God's billows had rolled over you, were you destroyed? Did they wash out your hope? Did your confidence give way? You once went down, as it were, into a very sea of trouble, and you thought you would have been drowned therein like Egypt of old. Did not the water-floods divide before you? Did not the depths stand upright as a heap, and were not the floods congealed in the heart of the sea?

You have had high mountains in your path, and you have said, "I can never traverse this road, the mountains are too steep." But have you not climbed them, and let me ask you have you not been benefited by the climb? When you have stood upon their lofty summit, has not the view of your knowledge become wider? Has not the breath of your prayer become purer, and freer? Have not your visits to the cold mountains of affliction strengthened you, and braced you for more glorious efforts than before?

Now, then, let the past console the future. Snatch a torch from the altars of the past, and rekindle the dying embers of today. He who has been with you in time past will not leave you in time to come. He is God; He changes not, He will not forsake you. He is God; He does not lie, He cannot leave you. He has sworn Himself, because He can swear by no greater, so that by two immutable things—His oath and His promise—we might have strong consolation, who have fled to the refuge to lay hold of the hope that is set before us. Though the barrel of meal hold but a scanty supply, though the cruse of oil contain but a drop, that meal shall last to the end, that cruse of oil, miraculously multiplied, hour by hour, shall be sufficient until you die, and with good old Jacob, end your life with a song, praising and blessing the angel who has redeemed you out of all evil.

Now, having thus addressed myself to the children of God, I hope to their comfort, I wish to say just a word or two to those whom I have come here with the hope of blessing this morning—those of you who know nothing of the love of God in Christ Jesus our Lord. What would you think of the condition of the man who can say, and say truly too, without a blush or stammer, "I know that I am the object of God's eternal love; I know that He has put all my sins behind His back, and that I stand before Him as accepted and as much beloved as if I had never sinned"? What would you say if that man could confidently add, "I know that this shall be my position in time and in eternity. God so loves me that He cannot cease to love me. He will preserve me whatever be my troubles or temptations, and I shall see His face, and shall rejoice in His love eternally"? Why, you answer, "If I could say that, I would give all that I am worth; if I were worth a thousand worlds I would give them all to say that."

Is it, then, an unattainable thing? Is it so high beyond your reach? I tell you, and the witness that I bear is true, there are tens of thousands of men on the face of God's earth who enjoy this state. Not always can they say as much, but still they enjoy it year after year continually. There are some of us who know what it is to have no doubt as to our eternal state. At times we tremble, but at other times we can say, "I know whom I have believed, and am persuaded that He is able to keep that which I have committed to him unto that day."

Again I hear you say, "Would to God I could say that." Well, my dear hearer, it is possible that you shall say it before long; no, tonight it may be, before sleep shall close your eyes, you may be among the happy men. "No," says one, "but I am the chief of sinners." Yes, but Christ is the Savior of the chief of sinners. "No," says another, "but my character is so bad, my disposition so evil." The Holy Spirit can change your disposition, can renew your will, and make you a new man in Christ. "Well," says a third, "I can understand that I may be pardoned, but I cannot think that I shall ever know it." That is the glory of the religion of Christ, that He not only forgives, but He tells you so: He sheds abroad in your heart a sweet consciousness of acceptance in Him; so that you know better than if an angel could tell you, that you are now one of the family of God, that all your sins are gone, and that every good thing is yours by an eternal covenant. Again, says a fourth, "I would that I could have it." Well, sinner, it is in your way. Do you feel and know yourself to be undeserving, ill-deserving, and hell-deserving? Then all that is asked of you is that you simply confess your sin to God; acknowledge that you are guilty, and then cast yourself flat on your face before the cross of Christ. He is able to save you, sinner, for He is able to save to the very uttermost all who come unto God by Him.

May God the Holy Spirit now send the word home, and may some who have been poor as the widow of Sarepta, now find a miraculous supply of grace through Jesus Christ our Lord! Amen.